DIANA
The Children's Princess

DIANA
The Children's Princess

Harriet Storey

Fawcett Columbine · New York

Designed and produced by
The Rainbird Publishing Group Ltd
40 Park Street, London W1Y 4DE

House editor: Rachel Stewart
Designer: Martin Bristow

A Fawcett Columbine Book
Published by Ballantine Books

Library of Congress Catalog Card Number: 84-90980

ISBN 0-449-90146-7

Manufactured in England
Text filmset by Bookworm Typesetting, Manchester
Color origination by Gilchrist Brothers Ltd, Leeds
Printed and bound by Ambassador Press Ltd, St Albans

First American Edition: December 1984
10 9 8 7 6 5 4 3 2 1

Front cover: *Diana chats happily to some children in New Zealand.*
Back cover: *The Prince of Wales, Diana and William in the gardens of
Kensington Palace, June 1984.*
Half-title: *The Princess of Wales cradles tiny Prince Harry in her arms
just one day after his birth in September 1984.*
Frontispiece: *Shy admirers meet the Princess of Wales in Wellington,
New Zealand.*

Illustration Acknowledgments

The publishers would like to thank the following who have supplied pictures
for reproduction in this book:

Mrs R.V.M. Anderson, New Malden: 90; Camera Press Ltd – Photo Patrick
Lichfield: 11; Colour Library International: 1, 23, 29, 57 (right), 58, 60, 61, 62, 65;
Tim Graham: 2, 7, 8, 9, 12, 13 (both), 14, 15 (both), 17, 19 (both), 20 (both), 21,
24-5, 26 (both), 28, 30-1, 32, 33, 34 (right), 35, 36 (both), 37, 38, 40, 41, 50, 54
(left), 59 (both), 63 (both), 69 (both), 70, 71, 72, 73, 74-5, 76, 77 (both), 78, 80,
81, 82, 85, 87, 88 (both), 89, 91 (top), 92, 93 (below), 95, 96 (both), front and
back covers; Anwar Hussein: 42, 43, 53, 57 (left), 67, 79; Rosie Oxley's Collection:
44-49; Photographers International: 34 (left), 39; Rainbird Picture Library: 93;
Rex Features: 27, 54 (right), 55; Russell Whitehurst, Yass, Australia: 91.

Contents

CHAPTER ONE

A Radiant Mother

Those who imagined that the fuss over the Princess of Wales' off-spring had reached its peak of hype and hysteria at the birth of her first child, Prince William, were disappointed on the 13 February 1984 when the Palace announced her second pregnancy. 'Secret Behind That Smile – A Baby!' enthused the *Daily Mail*. 'Smile That Says It All,' said the *Daily Express*. 'Happy Di Wants A Girl,' said the *Sun*, and the *Star* headlined the news 'September Baby For Diana And Charles – So Much In Love'.

To the unquenchable amazement of anti-monarchists, congratulatory crowds turned up outside Kensington Palace, the bookmakers' wires started buzzing and Sir Ronald Gardner-Thorpe who, as Lord Mayor of London at the time of the announcement of the Princess' first pregnancy, had come up with 'Babies are bits of stardust blown from the hand of God', rose to the occasion again with 'A lovely being scarcely formed or moulded; A rose with all its sweetest leaves unfolded.'

The timing of the announcement was perfect. As one royal observer said: 'Prince Charles and the Princess are so much in love they wanted to share their wonderful news for Valentine's Day with all the world's romantics.' But amongst the babble of baby talk, there was one voice of dissent. Professor Harold Francis, a senior gynaecologist at the Liverpool Women's Hospital, felt that if the Princess of Wales intended to have many more children, it could have catastrophic consequences. The 'baby boom' of the 60s, he gravely explained, was to be attributed partly to mothers following The Queen's example of four. The prospect of a 'Diana baby boom' he found horrifying. 'A third child would mean a crisis for the country, the obstetric service, the schools, and more importantly, the job situation,' he said. He even took it upon himself to suggest that the Prince and Princess should consider sterilization.

The last man who had hit the news with similar views on the evils of population growth was, ironically enough, Prince Philip, father of those very four, who on a visit to the Solomon Islands chose to air his views on their rapidly rising birth rate in the cheerful setting of a local maternity unit. 'Five per cent – five per cent – you must be out of your minds,' he said. 'You'll have a massive economic crisis in 20 years time and blame everybody else.'

According to the Palace, he did not share Professor Francis' doubts about the new royal infant. Nor did anyone else. At bus stops all over the country on the morning of 13 February the talk was not of the newly appointed Soviet leader, but of Diana's pregnancy. Politics were forgotten in the face of an important family event. For a royal marriage, death or birth are as important to the people of Britain as a marriage, death or birth in their own family.

In Russia, *Pravda* found the fuss made over Prince William sickening. 'If you sat close enough to the television you did not need sugar in your tea,' it reported, after the six-month-old Prince had been presented to

Right: Relaxed, and brimming with pleasure in each other's company, Diana and Prince William of Wales bring a new informal image to royal motherhood for the 1980s. The smiles were on the eve of the royal visit to Australia and New Zealand, when the Prince was only nine months old.

Above: Second son to the Prince and Princess of Wales and third in line to the throne, Prince Henry Charles Albert David (Harry for short) is presented to the world for the first time by his proud parents. Two years earlier, almost the same scene, featuring baby William, was enacted on the steps of St Mary's Hospital, Paddington (see page 17). As before, The Queen's Surgeon-Gynaecologist, Mr George Pinker, attended the birth. A little smaller than William, the baby weighed 6lb 14oz.

the cameras at Christmas 1982, adding that it would be better if the papers concentrated on the poor masses, which did not, like him, have a little silver boomerang to play with. In Britain, however, there is every evidence that 'the masses', poor and rich, are united in their delight at the sight of Prince William and his family, with or without silver boomerangs.

As *The Times* meditated in its leader at Christmas 1983: 'One of the functions of the monarchy in our national life is to represent the significance of family life. The circulation of nursery photographs and sentimental information about how the youngsters are coming on is as much a part of that function nationally as it is to the lives of any other family.' Anyone who doubts the strength of affection between the public and the monarchy need only watch the reactions of the crowds when a member of the Royal Family goes walkabout. Near hysterical enthusiasm at the approach of one of the Royals often gives way to tears of happiness on the part of those who have been spoken to – especially if the Royal concerned is The Queen or her daughter-in-law.

At the slightest hint of a problem in the royal household the nation weighs in with understanding and affection – in fact mothers identify so

Above: Prince William, with great concentration, practises his royal wave to the excited crowd which has gathered to see his new baby brother. He himself had just been introduced to little Prince Harry and there was a lot of laughter as he touched him and held his hand. Then Nanny Barbara Barnes took him home to Kensington Palace.

strongly with Diana that they write reassuringly to the papers, and to her, telling her not to worry about the things that once perplexed them. The intense interest in the Wales' domestic life suggest that Victorian family values are cherished as much today as they were in the nineteenth century.

If the representation of enduring family life is now one of the chief functions of constitutional monarchy, perhaps one of the reasons why the Princess of Wales, of all the members of the Royal Family, produces such an astonishing response, is that she manages to convey an image that combines the height of glamour with the most touching domesticity. Beautiful, rich and aristocratic by birth, she nevertheless makes it perfectly plain that for her, the ordinary job of being a wife and mother is what really counts.

The association in the mind of the public between Diana and children was made at the very moment the lady was first introduced to them as a likely future Queen of England, in that now legendary shot of her with the sun shining through her cotton skirt and a toddler on her hip. It splendidly summed up the combination of allure and maternal care that Diana has been projecting ever since. Before that moment no Fleet Street editor could ever have believed that such an image could hold more appeal and become more successful at selling papers than any page three siren.

Diana's arrival in the news came at the end of two decades when women had claimed headlines for their brazen sex appeal or for their success in their careers. Diana did not fit into either category. Her sex appeal is demure, alluring and unselfconscious – the very opposite of brazen. And her career achievements as a single girl were unspectacular. She was brought up in a highly conservative fashion in the old traditions of the British upper classes, with the emphasis in her education put on good manners, responsibility and the hope of a good husband, rather than good examination results. But she had no modern qualms about her role in life. From the moment of her engagement, when she appeared on television saying that with Charles to tell her what to do, she was sure she'd be all right, she revived the image of the nice, old-fashioned girl who had so long been out of the news. Her adoration for children was immediately obvious. She had worked as an assistant in the Young England kindergarten in Pimlico, and spent over a year looking after Patrick, the two-year-old son of an American couple. The public was instantly convinced that she was every mother's ideal daughter and every child's ideal mother.

From the way she picked up, cuddled and kissed the children she met on her post-engagement walkabouts, it was clear that her addiction to them was perfectly sincere. And she made no secret of the fact that she wanted lots of children of her own. Right from the very start, Diana really was the Children's Princess.

Her affinity with children was obviously one of the reasons Prince Charles chose her as his bride. He had already had a long list of girlfriends whose names read like a roll-call from Debrett's Peerage. Though all were suitable companions for an heir to the throne, only three really stood out as contenders for future Queen. These were

Davina Sheffield, Lady Sarah Spencer and the bookies' favourite, Lady Jane Wellesley.

As Charles' romances with these three cooled to friendship, attention turned to glamorous Princess Caroline and Catholic Princess Marie-Astrid, whose blue blood put them firmly in the running. But Charles ruled them out as incompatible. He knew just what he wanted: 'Marriage is a much more important business than falling in love... it's all about creating a secure family unit in which to bring up children. You have to remember that when you marry in my position, you're going to marry someone who is perhaps one day going to be Queen. You've got to choose someone very carefully, who could fill this particular role, and it has got to be someone pretty unusual.'

Charles also had to choose with exceptional care, because his is a marriage in which divorce is unthinkable, and as such an even more powerful symbol of family life than most. At the Royal Wedding on 29 July 1981 there was no room for cynical predictions, and the ceremony was lent even more poignancy by the sight of the Princess of Wales' divorced parents briefly united in St Paul's for their daughter's wedding. The wedding also reinforced, by its many child attendants, the link between the Princess of Wales and children. Apart from the famous kiss, one of the most charming moments on the balcony was the sight of Diana hand in hand with the youngest bridesmaid, Clementine Hambro, five years old, who had been one of her charges at the Young England kindergarten.

There was no doubt, right from the very first, that married life suited Diana down to the ground. Her honeymoon statement that marriage was wonderful – 'I highly recommend it' – was only to be hoped for from a bride of a few weeks, but even two years later in October 1983, when she met Barry Manilow at a charity concert at the Festival Hall, her talk was all of marriage and how much good it would do him. 'Get married and put some weight on,' she advised him. 'You really should have someone to look after you.' Even Barry was impressed by this concern. 'She was really sweet,' he told reporters later. 'She told me at least five times during our conversation that I ought to be married.'

The same enthusiasm was expressed in November 1982 to Margaret Younger, a resident of the Royal School for the Blind at Leatherhead, Surrey, when Diana called to open an extension. 'Married life is wonderful,' said the Princess, when she heard that Margaret was planning to marry another resident. Afterwards a delighted Miss Younger commented: 'That's the best advice anyone could have.' And Diana dished out more positive advice on a visit to Stoke Mandeville Hospital. 'Are you marrying?' she asked Mick Sorrell, who had been paralysed in a driving accident, when she saw him fondly talking to Wendy Hudson. When the couple seemed indecisive she told them briskly how splendid matrimony was. 'That', said Wendy, as she came out of the church door beneath a firemans' arch early in 1984, 'made up our minds. We had been thinking of getting married but after speaking to her we had no doubts left.'

On the subject of the bliss of marriage the Princess is indefatigable, which must be doing wonders for the ego of the Prince of Wales, if not for his figure. 'She keeps trying to feed me up,' he has been heard to say, confirming that her remarks to Mr Manilow were no jest.

When, a few months after the wedding, she became pregnant, her very evident pleasure, despite some alarm at the loss of her recently acquired slim figure and the unpleasantness of prolonged morning sickness, was in marked contrast to the attitude of her sister-in-law Princess Anne the year before when she was pregnant with Zara. There was a critical reaction to Anne's typically ironic, self-deprecatory remarks in a 40-minute television documentary, which showed her with Captain Phillips in their Gatcombe Park home. 'I'm not particularly maternal in outlook,' she said, playing down her obvious affection for young Peter and her astonishing and tireless commitment to the Save The Children Fund. She thought that the main part of her pregnancy was 'a very boring six months' and added wryly: 'It's an occupational hazard if you're a wife.'

Next day righteous indignation ran loose among the press, placing unwarranted interpretations on Anne's remarks and demanding to know what right a privileged Princess had to sneer at motherhood when there were so many unfortunate women around who would give anything to be in the state she found so boring.

There was no chance of misinterpreting the Princess of Wales' attitude to pregnancy. From the beginning her delight was evident. And, from the beginning, because William had been conceived so soon after

Below: Always surrounded by children, Diana made no exception for her wedding, where she starred in the midst of five bridesmaids and two pageboys. Here five-year-old Clementine Hambro, great-granddaughter of Sir Winston Churchill, and one of the children Diana had looked after in the Pimlico kindergarten, receives a quick word of reassurance before the balcony scene on the wedding day.

her marriage, while public interest in her was still insatiable, the Princess of Wales became the first member of the Royal Family to have a highly media-visible pregnancy.

Every trace of paleness, every sign of morning sickness was anxiously reported and overnight, gynaecologists became sibyls, to be questioned at every stage for pronouncements about whether the Princess was under too much stress, whether it was wise for her to have a home birth, and – inevitably – what the chances were of her having twins.

So keen was the public's interest in Diana that reporters and photographers, including the legendary James Whitaker, were despatched to crawl through the undergrowth of the Caribbean to catch sight of the pregnant Princess in her bikini. Charles and Diana were staying at the house of Lord Mountbatten's grandson, Lord Romsey, on the island of Windermere. After a dash through the jungle with the film and the story, where by his own account Mr Whitaker showed courage and resilience against near impossible odds which would have done justice to a hardened war reporter, the blurred and highly unflattering shots were wired back to London to appear next day in the *Sun*, while another set, taken from a few yards away, were published in the *Star*. The papers sold out, and an outcry resulted. There was general agreement that this was taking an interest in the royal domestic life and the Princess' pregnancy too far.

More decorous photographs of the pregnant Princess appeared right up to the last few days before she gave birth – unthinkable at the time of The Queen's pregnancies. Her last public engagement, five weeks before the birth, was to open the Albany Community Centre in Deptford. And Diana's appearance in those later months, when she continued to look both glamorous and healthy, was a marvellous proof that expectant mothers today need not feel pregnancy is a shameful and disfiguring state. The Princess more than lived up to the challenge to appear at her best. It was not just her tall figure that helped her to look so good, though a height of 5' 10" was no disadvantage. She managed, when she assembled her wardrobe for the crucial six months, not to fall into the trap of buying the usual apologetic flowery smocks, but instead adapted her own style to her new shape.

Her low pumps were already ideal for pregnancy, and so were the deep white sailor collars and big artists' bows she had made into a trademark from the beginning. Like her chokers, they focussed attention on her face. In a series of clear, fresh-coloured silk day dresses from

Below left: In the last months the Princess of Wales, suntanned and cheerful, was visibly delighting in the imminent prospect of a baby. 'I'm hoping for a boy,' she told a questioner in the crowd on 18 May 1982 when she opened the Albany Community Centre – her last public engagement before William's birth.
Below right: Relaxed and in the pink for a visit to a game of polo at Smith's Lawn, Windsor, in June. She chose her famous gold 'D' pendant to go with a dress which unblushingly drew attention to her pregnancy.

Left: The children of St Mary's were so pleased to see the Duchess of Cornwall on her April visit to the Scilly Isles in 1982 that they gave her no less than 74 posies.
Above left: Witty and comfortable – Diana gives new inspiration to maternity fashion in her koala jumper at a polo match in May.
Above right: Very simple lines, eye-catching detail at the neck and on the hat, and sensibly low heels for Diana's appearance at Ascot in June.

favourite designers such as Belville Sassoon and Jasper Conran, she looked wonderful, especially as, in the last few months, she was deeply sun-tanned and glowing with happiness.

Crowds thrilled to see her flouting the tradition of 'confinement' and turning up on the first day of Royal Ascot – a mere six days before the birth – in yards of palest peach and a pillbox, looking stunning. She solved the problem of being pregnant in formal evening dress by choosing historically inspired gowns from a period when fuller figures were the rage, like the Stuart style deep red taffeta gown Belville Sassoon made for her, with a high waist, low neckline and lace at neck and cuffs, which she wore, glittering with diamonds, at the Barbican Arts Centre in March. By proving so convincingly that pregnancy need not be a dowdy state, Diana did every woman a service.

But perhaps she looked most engaging of all informally clad for one of Charles' polo engagements, in an enormous, brightly coloured sweater with a koala bear design, which was knitted for her husband by an Australian fan. It was an inspired and an inspiring choice. A popular paper ran a knitting pattern of it and maternity wear buyers began looking around for a good supplier of bright, amusing knitwear. Fun, something long missing from most maternity wear shops, was suddenly fashionable. Instead of concealing it, the koala bear woolly drew attention to the Princess' bump. Once again, Diana started a new trend in fashion, this time appealing additionally to the many women who now choose to have their first child at a later age, and are thrilled by the prospect of pregnancy instead of taking it as a matter of course.

At five a.m. on 21 June 1982 the nation was on tenterhooks as the Princess of Wales was driven with her husband to St Mary's Hospital, Paddington. She was in the early stages of labour and was admitted to a special room in the Lindo Wing. Her baby was the first heir to the throne to be born in hospital.

Outside the building crowds of wellwishers and press gathered, and they stayed the whole day despite a continual drizzle. The Princess' labour lasted 16 hours, and Charles was at her side throughout. He was present at the birth of their son at 9.03 that evening, Midsummer's Day. Diana's gynaecologist, George Pinker, confirmed that it had been a nearly natural birth. 'Yes it was ... well, almost. Just at the end the Princess did have a bit of pain relief, but I'm afraid I can't go into details.' The baby's father was overwhelmed by the event and admitted, on his emergence from the hospital, that being a father was 'rather a grownup thing. Rather a shock to my system.'

At Buckingham Palace the traditional notice announcing the arrival of the second in line to the throne was posted behind the gates. William weighed 7lb 1½oz, cried lustily and had a wisp of fair hair and blue eyes. Inside the Palace his royal grandparents celebrated with champagne, while telegrams bearing the news of the birth were sent to the four corners of the earth. The Archbishop of Canterbury, Dr Robert Runcie, proclaimed: 'We rejoice with them. It is good news for millions around the world who hold them in their affection and their prayers.' And The Queen ordered a personal tribute of two 41-gun salutes to be fired at one o'clock the following day.

Before their short stay in hospital was over, Diana and her son were visited by her parents, Mrs Shand Kydd and Earl Spencer. 'She is looking radiant, absolutely radiant,' said Diana's mother. 'My grandson is a lovely baby. There is a great deal of happiness in there.' The Princess' father enthused: 'He is the most beautiful baby I have ever seen.'

The modern mother began as she meant to go on, leaving hospital only 36 hours after her arrival to a tumultuous reception from the crowds outside. As the couple appeared on the steps of the Lindo Wing, Charles passed the baby to his wife. The gesture was perfect. They were a family.

Only a year later, while the country was reaffirming its enthusiasm for Diana's firstborn by sending over 1000 birthday cards to a Prince at the tearing rather than the reading stage, and Charles was celebrating with a cake that weighed more than the boy himself, royal watchers were already speculating on a new pregnancy for the Princess.

The game had begun the month before William's birthday, when on the authority of no less a person than Prince Charles' ex-valet, Stephen Barry, gossip columnist Nigel Dempster announced that if she were not

Above: Some day my prince will come – Diana and Charles, the day after the baby prince arrived, leaving St Mary's Hospital, Paddington for Kensington Palace.

already pregnant, she would become so by the autumn. Earl Spencer nurtured the rumour by hoping out loud that all three of his daughters would present him with a new grandchild that year. But talk of what was excrutiatingly called 'a nappy event' did not really take off until June, when Prince Charles made an unfortunate public joke about 'the royal breeding programme'. It was, he said, 'firmly underway'.

The Palace switchboard was besieged. Official statements that the remark was merely humorous were not helped a few days later at a Windsor polo match, when Chief Inspector Colin Trimming, asked why Diana was not with Charles, stepped out of his role as personal detective and into that of court jester with his response: 'This morning sickness does terrible things to you.'

It was probably less of a joke to the Princess herself, who found all eyes on her waistline. A few pounds on, a trace of a smile, and flickering interest about her 'pregnancy' became a forest fire. But if she *lost* a few pounds and became super-slim, the word went round that Diana, like her sister Sarah before her, was annorexic and therefore, rumour impertinently concluded, probably unable to have a baby. Diana put her own foot in it days after the polo joke when she visited a hospital in Preston and made headlines once more by innocently asking if there was a German measles epidemic there. 'The disease can harm unborn children if the mother comes into contact with it early in pregnancy,' reported the *Daily Express* significantly.

Speculation died down over the summer, but by autumn, with the excitement of the Canadian tour and William's first birthday over, the public and the papers were ready for another guessing game. It was given the perfect start when the Princess flew back from Balmoral for a day early in September, just as she had done at the start of her first pregnancy two years previously. It happened to be on the same day that her gynaecologist returned to work from his holidays. Speculation ran rife, but the real reason for the Princess' trip was a mundane one – she was en route to her hairdresser, Kevin Shanley.

In the ensuing though unwarranted hubbub, members of the public proved that they too were interested in playing the part of amateur gynaecologist and pregnancy spotter. 'We are very curious to know if you are having a baby,' said a factory girl called Elaine Robertson when she met Diana at the Keiller marmalade and sweet plant in Dundee. And the papers, desperate for any straws in the wind, turned to that old standby, 'women's intuition', for confirmation. They were delighted when Elaine declared firmly that the Princess was pregnant. Valerie Gowans, aged 26, agreed. 'Definitely,' she said, cuddling her seven-month-old daughter Jennifer. The Princess, she pointed out, was not only 'gorgeous' but 'blooming', a sure sign that another little Wales was on the way. Elaine's declaration was pounced upon by James Whittaker, the royal journalist extraordinaire. Using a considerable amount of imagination, he described a party to celebrate the news of her new pregnancy. 'The Royal Family were delighted and called for champagne to celebrate,' he wrote. 'I am told there was a lot of kissing at the same time, followed by a very jolly dinner party.'

Diana's cross press secretary Victor Chapman immediately issued a firm denial. Nevertheless the rumours continued into October. By November there were speculations on the chance of twins in 1984, on the grounds that Diana's aunt on her father's side had had them, her grandmother on her mother's side was one of a pair, and her aunt on the same side had also produced a double. The mere idea of the amount of extra attention the arrival of the first pair of royal twins for centuries would produce is so exhausting that it is more than probable Charles and Diana were *not* hoping for them.

In January 1984 the papers did an about-turn. Tired of the craze for baby-spotting, they now began to explain why the Princess was intending *not* to have another baby for quite some time. 'At the moment she is still not quite confident enough to commit herself to anything which would separate her from her husband, even temporarily,' reported the *News of the World*. In fact the Princess of Wales had fooled them all and shown her confidence and her commitment in her own way, by becoming pregnant just 'when everyone was least expecting it', as her brother, 19-year-old Charles, Viscount Althorp proudly put it. He added that it was well known in the family that she wanted another child quickly.

The news that 'the royal breeding programme' really was underway was received with great delight, not least by the workers at the Jaguar car plant in Coventry, where the royal couple made their first public appearance together after Buckingham Palace had made the announcement. When Prince Charles complimented bench worker Terry McCauley on the state of affairs at the car company: 'You're doing very good work here, production is going well,' he was taken aback to receive congratulations in return. 'Your production line is going well too,' said Mr McCauley. Blushing amidst the laughter, Charles attempted to cover his confusion with a goodbye line: 'Keep up the good work,' only to be told: 'You and all, mate.' And in token of Jaguar's approval of the production line at Kensington Palace, they began work on a special new product – a one-off modelled down Jaguar pedal car for Prince William's second birthday to match the one Charles had ordered for himself on his February visit.

Humour has never been lacking from the affection the British show for their Royals. No sooner had the news of Diana's pregnancy been announced, than a bookie offered odds of 1000 to 1 on the name 'Spike',

Below left: Diana and her young son go walking to meet the press in the garden of Kensington Palace – and for once it is William's dress, not his mother's, the fashion pundits have their eyes on.
Below right: A modern addition to the traditional royal calendar of duties and pleasures – the annual skiing trip Charles and Diana take. They were staying with the royal family of Liechtenstein.

Above left: The twentieth-century prince arrives by air in Auckland, safe in the arms of nanny Barbara Barnes.

Above right: The royal baby has pretty painted furniture in his nursery at Kensington Palace.

after Charles' favourite comedian, Spike Milligan. Milligan was the man who entertained the Prince at the Lyric Theatre with jokes about his sister, her husband and Barbara Cartland, summing up the evening with an updated version of the National Anthem: 'God save our gracious Queen, Prince Philip, Charles, Di and the kid'.

Only Charles and Diana know how large they would like their family to be, but the public cannot help speculating that Diana might follow the example of her predecessor Alexandra, Princess of Wales, and have seven children without producing any more serious consequences to the populace – despite the fears of professors of demography – than a great deal of pleasure and a quantity of souvenir booklets. The desire for a large family is not the only thing that unites these two Princesses of Wales. Despite the helicopters on the lawns and the mass of security gadgets surrounding her residences, Diana's whole life is far closer to that of Alexandra's a full century ago than it is to many of her subjects. In Diana's home Alexandra would find the household rather shrunk, perhaps, but still familiar. The lady's maid, Evelyn Dagley, the one-time Buckingham Palace parlourmaid who was promoted to caring for Diana's huge wardrobes of taffeta ballgowns, silken day dresses, jaunty small veiled hats and neat kid shoes, wears jeans instead of a starched apron and grey dress, but she deals with a wardrobe not dissimilar in its contents and uses from Alexandra's own.

There are still nannies in the nursery – Barbara Barnes, also less formally dressed than she would have been a century ago, but still performing much the same role, with the help of an under nanny, Mrs Olga Powell. Diana might bath her babies herself to the sound of rock music on the radio, but the nursery staff make it possible for her to be a

A Radiant Mother

working mother. The recent butler, Manchester-born Mr Alan Fisher, enlivened his traditional role at the door of Diana's Kensington Palace home by greeting visitors in sneakers beneath his pin stripes, a habit he claims to have picked up while working for Bing Crosby. Alexandra would also be familiar with the concept of a country residence, Highgrove House near Tetbury, with its capacious grounds and land (348 acres), horses in the stables and fine works of art on the walls, though the swimming pool would not have been there in her day. The Wales' apartment in Kensington Palace may have a fine Georgian staircase and ample accommodation for a small family and staff, but it is still not as fine as the house in which Alexandra entertained when she was Princess of Wales in Victoria's reign. The heir to the throne and his wife, who was as famous throughout the land for her love of children as Diana is today, occupied the majestic Marlborough House near St James' Palace, a stone's throw away from Clarence House, so familiar to our Princess as the residence of her grandmother-in-law.

Even Diana's social calendar is based on the same fixed paths as Alexandra's: Ascot in June, Cowes in August, Scotland in autumn – the same Balmoral with its tartan carpets, where Diana's children will learn, as Alexandra's did, the traditional sports of hunting, shooting and

Below: Prince Charles took a keen interest in his son long before his birth, according to Diana, who claimed he was reading too many books on babies and was telling her what to do. His close involvement with his children's early years is thoroughly modern – and a great change from the days when royal fathers only saw their children for a few minutes a day, and then safely guarded by nannies. This family photograph was taken just before the Australian tour, in their Kensington Palace apartment. The wallpaper is printed with the Prince of Wales' feathers.

fishing. The January skiing trips and yearly visits to the Caribbean are modern, though equally regular additions to the Princess of Wales' calendar. These jaunts further afield would not surprise the fun-loving Alexandra as much as the batteries of cameras outside Diana's gate and the Sony headphones and rollerskates she is said to wear. Diana moves with the times, but the job description of the Princess of Wales has altered very little.

It is probably partly because her role is steeped in tradition that the Princess is seen as such an attractive figure. In a crinoline skirt and a Saudi prince's ransom in diamonds and sapphires she looks just like everybody's idea of a romantic Princess from a historical novel come to life. There is not much enthusiasm in Britain for the pedestrian sort of royalty found elsewhere on the Continent, and that is something else the Princess seems to sense instinctively. Both her job and her person symbolise tradition, and this is what her people want.

Even Prince William hardly looked like a child of his time when he was first displayed for the camera. Clad in the hand-smocked silks his mother chose for the occasion, he bore a closer resemblance to the Prince Charles of 35 years before, than to most of his contemporaries, crawling about in their brightly coloured stretch romper suits. The similarity between father and son underlined the continuity in the Royal Family: this baby was special, and no-one wanted to pretend otherwise.

The appeal of William and his mother is so special, in fact, that to be a member of the aristocracy, a stratum of society that was despised and ignored throughout the 1960s, has suddenly become highly fashionable, and the style of the so-called Sloane Ranger is now immensely popular and much copied. The Princess of Wales has been christened the Super-Sloane, but under this new name lies the age-old fascination with aristocracy that Diana has made respectable again to the middle classes. Twenty years ago it was suppressed. A hundred years ago there was no pretence about it.

This return to fashion has meant that Prince Charles, who seemed so out of place in the 60s in his brogues and tweeds and earnest attitudes, has suddenly found himself in his maturity to be a man of his times. And the return to an emphasis on the importance of traditional values is a return to his own views, solidly rooted as they are in a conservative approach to institutions, liberal ideals, and an absolute conviction of the necessity of a solid family life. Charles' family life is deeply rooted in history and William, who is by all accounts a forceful baby, has brought this home to his father more clearly than ever before. Charles described it like this: 'Suddenly you find that your child is not a malleable object or an offprint of yourself, but is the culmination of goodness knows how many thousands of years and genetic make-up of your ancestors.'

In his knowledge of his own children's thousands of years of genetic make-up the Prince is undoubtedly uniquely well placed. But in his appreciation of each child's unique preciousness he is voicing the sentiments of every parent. The way people identify with the Wales family is the reason why there is, and will continue to be, such a tremendous response to the Children's Princess and the Princess' children.

Right: Sparkling, despite a second pregnancy which she found very tiring from its earliest stages, Diana dressed for evening in an historically inspired gown with high waist, low neckline and detailed sleeves which are very flattering in maternity.

CHAPTER TWO

A Way with Children

From the first moment Lady Diana Spencer went walkabout, after the announcement of her engagement to the Prince of Wales, it was clear that children were her first love. Photographs showed Diana breaking through the formality that had up till then existed even on informal walkabouts. Spontaneous, charming, obviously happy, she was seen crouching on the ground, silk skirts trailing in the dirt, chatting to toddlers, hugging small ice-cream besmeared brats who held up their arms to her, coo-ing over babies, and swapping jokes with 10-year-olds as though the whole lot of them were a set of small cousins she hadn't seen for a few days.

To the surprise of some observers, the spectacle continued. A hundred walkabouts later the fully fledged Princess, who had learned how to stand on her dignity with the press, was kissing and cuddling the nation's children with an enthusiasm that showed she was as besotted as ever. Now the line of tiny royal fans below handshake-level is such a familiar sight that it is hardly remarked on. They all clutch posies wrapped in silver foil, and the Princess will gratefully accept them, or coax one from an unwilling hand if the giver is overcome with stage-fright. The children know that they will be the first to receive Diana's attention – and to make absolutely certain of it, they will spend hours crayoning in bright banners 'We love you, Princess Di', or the name of their school, with a message of welcome.

Even those who work with children are delighted and amazed by the natural rapport Diana has with them. A typical comment came after her visit to the Great Ormond Street Hospital for Sick Children in December 1982. 'She was absolutely marvellous with the children and the staff loved her,' said the House Governor, Mr Bill Milchen. 'She is so very natural. She has a way with children that is truly fantastic.' Mr Milchen was expressing his conversion to the huge multitude of Diana's fans. And their hearts are touched not only by her strong maternal instincts, but also by the shyness she felt when she was first on public display.

With the world's cameras on her, a posse of policemen at her heels, and thousands of strangers scrutinizing her every movement, the 19-year-old Lady Diana Spencer took refuge in talking to those with whom she felt most at ease: children. Before her marriage she had had little outward success. She had not shone at school, or in finding a job she liked enough to stick at afterwards. And despite her strong character and insatiable interest in people, there had been very little in her life to build up her confidence in her abilities. In all probability, shyness as well as kindness lay behind her request on her first visit to the school at Tetbury, to skip coffee with the teachers so that she could spend more time with the children. A heartfelt gesture, no doubt, and one that was much appreciated. But the thought of speaking to adults in awe of her position and putting them at their ease must have been more terrifying for a teenager unused to her role than chatting with children. With

Above: On the streets of Tetbury, in May 1981, the then Lady Diana Spencer showed the informality and love of children which were to be the hallmark of royal walkabouts thereafter. Above right: Knee-level talks at Broadlands at a tree planting ceremony. This habit of conversing at grassroots took security men by surprise on Diana's first public appearances with her husband-to-be.

Previous page: Flags and flowers and a row of small hands at every level – familiar sights at each Diana walkabout. This one was in Canberra during her Australian tour.

children she could be herself, because they would be completely themselves with her.

Her confidence with children was securely based. From her earliest years, when she had helped look after her baby brother Charles, she had demonstrated her talents in that direction. Before her engagement she had worked as an unpaid nanny for friends, as well as at the Young England kindergarten. At school at West Heath near Sevenoaks she used to go for one afternoon a week to a home for the handicapped to play with the children and help out the busy staff. She also used to call each week on an old lady to do her shopping and help around the house, and it was noticeable that, after children, Diana sought out the old to chat to as comfortable and familiar friends. Once she began to accept engagements on her own account, homes for old people as well as children's hospitals and homes became a priority on her official schedule. The Princess of Wales is the Chelsea Pensioners' favourite pin-up. 'Forget Vera Lynn, forget Lilian Gish,' said 84-year-old RSM John McLellan when she visited the Royal Hospital in December 1983, 'the Princess of Wales has taken over.'

The love between Diana and the people began because both sides needed and wanted each other. And a great part of the reason for Diana's success with young and old is that the affection is kept on an equal footing. The toddlers are hugged and kissed in a way which suggests that it is as much a treat for her as it is for them. Diana avoids the

Right: The Princess of Wales meets a young Welshman on her visit to Brecon after her honeymoon. Moments later he received one of those precious royal kisses that children were beginning to clamour for.

run of patronizing adult questions about names and ages, and what they will do when they're grown up. Instead she drops down from her 5' 10" to eye-level contact – her long full skirts must often be chosen with her small fans in mind – and swaps information. She teases and sympathises: 'I wasn't much good at music, I couldn't cope with sight-reading,' she told one child when she visited the Children's Youth Orchestra in April 1984. She shows she understands about the difficulties of being bossed by elder sisters. She has been known to ask for a fruit gum, even a loan. 'Can I have your 10p to get me home?' she asked an appalled three-year-old on her tour of Great Ormond Street Hospital, and grinned as Ben Walford stoutly refused to hand over his cash.

With her pregnancy and the birth of William she found another group with whom she achieved instant rapport. 'Oh the joy of things to come!' she said enviously to a mother holding her young baby in her arms in the Scilly Isles, and once the joy had duly arrived she was chatting to all the mothers she came across about the difficulties of teething problems and of bringing up children, in a way which quite brushed aside any embarrassment they might have had speaking to a Princess. She has an invaluable gift for identifying with those she meets, no doubt partly because she has not suffered from the handicap of being born a princess, distant and apart. And though she was at first shy of public functions, possible mishaps, and public speaking, she was never in the slightest bit embarrassed when children broke protocol. A laugh was

Above: Gloveless in spite of the cold, the Princess of Wales delightedly greets two small and well muffled admirers in Oslo. The news of her second pregnancy was yet to be announced.

her only response when a three-year-old tried to pull her hat off at a visit to a hospital in Wrexham.

When she called for tea at a former council flat on the Easterhouse estate in Glasgow, she was more at ease than her hostess. 'I expect I'll be vacuuming and dusting right up to the last moment,' said Mrs Helen McAllen on the eve of her call. 'The children make such a mess.' When the Princess settled down on the sofa with her cup of weak tea and a sliver of strawberry gateau the dreaded happened. Two-year-old Barry moved in. 'I'm afraid that Barry tried to eat the Princess's cake as she was having her tea,' said his mother, 'but she coped beautifully.' Diana posed for a photograph for the family album with the rest of the children afterwards.

For the children, she is the stuff of fairy tales, appearing as if by magic in their street, good, beautiful, kind, and fond of them, as princesses are supposed to be. Perhaps because like them she once dreamed about princesses herself, Diana quite understands how her young fans see her. Five-year-old Samantha Markby, who went to see the Princess in Camberley in 1982, put it like this: 'I like Princess Diana because she's beautiful and she smiles a lot. I'd like to tell her I love her. I think Princess Diana is like a fairy Princess. I'd like to blow her a kiss but I can't send it because I don't know where she is and it would get lost.'

The occasional child might be disappointed because she is not actually carrying a wand, but Diana is aware that a good number fully

Above: Despite the officialdom and pomp surrounding every visit, Diana somehow manages to make each child she talks to feel she has her full, natural, and special attention. This time she is at the Fisher Price Toy Factory at Peterlee in County Durham.

Overleaf: Red roses for 'I love you' – children give them to Diana wherever she goes. Here it is a small girl in the crowd at the Hearsay Centre in Catford.

expect to see her dressed with diamonds in broad daylight. On a visit to Carlisle she apologized to eight-year-old Gerald Beedle for wearing her fetching little grey tip-tilted hat instead of a crown, 'He has dirty sticky hands,' said Gerald's teacher in warning, as the child stretched out his arms to touch her, but the warning went ignored, as usual. Diana is not shy of contact and more often than not goes without gloves. She once gave back a glove a three-year-old had dropped on the road with the comment: 'It's a vital piece of equipment in this weather.' But though it was chilly, the Princess herself was barehanded. The reason she does not follow the example of her mother-in-law – the Queen wears gloves for walkabouts even in tropical climes – may have something to do with the tradition set when she was Lady Diana Spencer and every child and its mother wanted to see the sapphire engagement ring. But it probably has more to do with her desire to cut down the barriers of formality between herself and the children who welcome her.

She will be seen straightening a child's crooked tie, or coaxing a fallen red wellington boot back onto a little foot with a cheerful 'Musn't let your tootsies get cold!', or admonishing a shy toddler: 'Don't suck your thumb, or your teeth will fall out!' Amidst all the pomp and ceremony, it is the Princess who notices when things are going wrong: it was she who spotted a boy being crushed against a crowd barrier on a visit to Newcastle in March 1982. 'I got my legs stuck against a crush bar as the crowd pushed forward. I fell down, but the next thing I knew

Above: Is there anybody there? Yes – Diana had spotted the tiny hand which indicated that there was an anxious child trying to see her through the bars, during the second day of her visit to Wales, at Carmarthen.

Princess Di was picking me up. She asked me if I was all right. I said I was. She was lovely, really smashing,' said an infatuated 10-year-old.

Apologizing and sympathizing are two of her chat-up techniques. She's constantly asking children how long they've spent waiting for her and worrying about how cold they must be. The girl who 'tried hard' at school and won a special award for service because of her cheerful personality and genuine interest in other people hasn't changed. When she heard that a posy presenter had caught chicken pox and missed his big chance to see her she was careful to send her best wishes and a surprise present to cheer up his sick bed. 'The Princess has been lovely about it,' said his father, David Ainscough, a fork-lift truck driver at a toy factory in Peterlee. 'It's typical of her.'

It was typical of the Princess too that the staff of the Royal Hospital for Sick Children in Glasgow did not need to point out to her the hopeful child standing pleadingly by the door, who had suffered from spina bifida all her life and scarcely knew her real home as well as she knew the hospital. Diana spotted 11-year-old Margaret McSharry straight away and instantly knelt to talk to her. 'I will remember it for the rest of my life,' said Margaret. And it is typical of the Princess to respond delightedly when a child breaks through the security barriers, as she did when three-year-old Colin Griffiths caught her and asked for a kiss outside the pagoda she was opening with Charles in April 1982, when she was pregnant. The kissers are just as welcome when they come in muddy

Below: Diana is now expert at the art of coaxing bouquets from the hands of shy children – like this little boy, who handed over his flowers after she and Charles had been planting trees in Hyde Park, London, to commemorate their marriage .

boots, like six-year-old Andrew Harrison's, which left their mark on Diana when she visited a playground for handicapped children in Gloucestershire. The sight of Diana touring playgrounds and schools with a toddler clinging tightly to each hand is not an unusual one.

With Diana, children get away with liberties no one else would dare take. In the middle of speculation over a possible second pregnancy in

September 1983, 13-year-old Fiona Passmore, a girl at a centre for mentally handicapped children and adults in Bedfordshire, patted her stomach and asked her: 'How's the baby?' and got a smile and a gentle 'Did I hear right?' from the Princess. And though she may deliberately avoid press cameras, remaining unrepentantly sullen as she did at a carol service after her return from the Bahamas and the notorious bikini-picture episode, she will always smile for a child's instamatic, and a cry of 'Mummy, take the picture now!' will halt her in her steps as it did on a visit to Deptford, when a little girl broke loose from the crowd to pose hopefully by her skirts.

When the grown-ups have gone, and the photographers disappeared, she will play monsters with the children she visits in homes and hospitals, join in their sing-songs, help them draw pictures, and admire their toys. There is no doubt where her loyalties lie – and it is not with the publicity machine. Nevertheless, her warmth and sweetness of nature have helped greatly to make her a super-star, a girl who is seen to be spoilt neither by mass publicity nor high rank, a Princess who lives up to the ideals in the poem Victorian children used to learn by heart: 'If you can talk with crowds and keep your virtue, Or walk with Kings – nor lose the common touch.'

That common touch, which is so endearing, is a gift the Princess also seems to have magically bestowed, by her presence, on Prince Charles.

Below left: There's a whole lot of lovin' going on – in Liverpool, which Diana visited during her first pregnancy.
Below right: Towards the end of his wife's pregnancy Charles began to take a keen interest in the small babies he came across. He met this baby girl in April in St Mary's, Scilly Isles.

From the moment of the balcony kiss on their wedding day it was evident that the previously rather stiff, slightly formal Prince of Wales was changing his public style. On the walkabouts that followed their engagement they were seen to be evolving a special public double-act, chatting together over children in the crowd, with Diana giving Charles a bit of aid with the babies, and Charles supporting Diana through the tricky moments of public speeches and formal introductions. Though at the beginning the Prince had some problems remembering to insert 'we' into his speeches where 'I' had done before, he rapidly discovered that the public had no difficulties in remembering Diana was with him. He also discovered, very obviously, that guiding Diana through the protocol was fun. Chatting with the children was simplicity itself with Diana around, with jokes flying between them. 'How's the old arm?' he asked young Jonathan Wareham, whose left wrist was in plaster when they visited the Cheshire Regiment stationed in Hampshire before the wedding. 'He probably did it chasing the girls!' chipped in his fiancée.

Joint visits with Diana were expanded to take in more contact with babies, mothers and schoolchildren, and the newly married Prince soon found himself in a maternity ward, gravely discussing birth and babies with the mothers and pronouncing on what a good thing it was, this idea of having fathers present at the birth. The Prince, who had been famous for keeping his hands firmly clasped behind his back, was

Right: Not all the kisses were for Diana. Children caught on to the idea that other members of her family might be in need of affection too. Charles in the grasp of a royalist at Liverpool, when the two of them visited the Cammell Laird apprentice training school.

Above left: Children who fail to pick the side of the street Diana walks down make the best of it by giving their flowers to Charles to give to her. His role as second best gives him much wry amusement.

Above right: Not just the children can be pretty sure to catch Diana's eye. Those in wheelchairs are almost always singled out for a word too. An exchange of greetings at Rhyl, North Wales.

pictured with babies in his arms, his look of anticipation giving way later to a confident smile. He was seen with his arm round his wife, kissing her hand in public at the Braemar Games, and patting her encouragingly on the bottom in a possessive kind of way. Suddenly small children, like 11-year-old Geoffrey Johnson at a joint visit to a centre for handicapped children in Liverpool, were running forward to hug *him* as well as his wife. Glory and glamour were reflected onto him, and the earnestly responsible, thoughtful, well-informed speeches he gives gained extra credibility simply because his wife has the gift of demonstrating, by direct action and simple questions, the genuine care for people they both feel.

The public speeches show that Charles and Diana share a special concern for the problems of the young and the old, a concern well demonstrated when the royal pair were guests at the 125th anniversary dinner of the Jewish Welfare Board in London, and Charles had on his mind the case of an aged widow left bleeding in her garden after an attack by two young muggers. 'We badly need to discover the meaning of this supposedly old-fashioned value which recognizes old age and accords it the respect it deserves,' he said, while the Princess sat beside him. 'Young people seem to despise the old. Often they think nothing of beating them up, outside or inside their homes, just for the pension books they can pick up... What do we do about it, we who pride ourselves on being a civilized society?'

Interest in the tragic problems faced by the old in a society where the family no longer plays the strong part in looking after them it once did is balanced by Prince Charles' deep interest in the difficulties faced by the young. What he attempts to do about it, in his own words, is to understand the problems at their root, and give some practical assistance to put things right in his administration of the Jubilee Trust, set up to help young people, and particularly young people in difficult areas. His interest in youth, and his wife's interest in very young children – her favourite age group, as she once told play group leader Caroline Ritchie, is pre-school infants – go excellently in tandem.

That Charles and Diana share these interests even in their private moments was made clear when he arrived on a visit to Stoke Mandeville Hospital triumphantly and unexpectedly bringing Diana with him. 'The atmosphere and spirit here is quite extraordinary,' he said. 'I mentioned this to my wife and she thought what I had to say was interesting, so she said she would come along as well.' And they went on to tour the hospital in their usual complementary style, Charles asking the detailed questions on administration and expenses, and Diana chatting to all and sundry, lifting everyone's spirits, and now and then shooting in a penetratingly simple question that went right to the heart of the matter.

From the beginning, their joint engagements were arranged to make a special point of including children and young people as much as possible. Their post-honeymoon visit to Wales, for example, was timed to coincide with half-term holidays. The sound of children's voices raised in Welsh songs and poems, in shouts and cheers of welcome, was the leit motif of that tour. In Caernarvon Castle, as the Prince presented Diana to her people and the two of them listened to local children singing in Welsh about Noah's Ark, they must have been thinking of their own secret – that the Principality was to have yet another Prince or Princess of Wales in a short time.

Below: On the Welsh tour, at Rhyl, Diana finds the one small face which is not smiling at her – too overcome by the fuss and the effort of handing over those roses, perhaps.

Above: A gaggle of small tilted faces in front, a posse of photographers tilting their lenses behind – a familiar sight on the Princess' appearance, this time in Wandsworth, London.

For the children of Wales and the rest of Britain, Charles and Diana make history come alive. Abstract ideas about the indefinable role of a constitutional monarchy are dull and difficult things for children to grasp. Stability, continuity, nationality, are grown-up words. In the attitudes and actions of Charles and Diana, in the scrapbooks of their visits and their parents' tales of former kings and queens, these concepts suddenly achieve reality. For the children of Tetbury school who designed a first birthday card for Prince William, monarchy is explained in terms of the pretty girl who has twice called to play and ask them all about themselves. The future of the institution seems less in doubt than ever with such a couple as tomorrow's King and Queen.

But the future Queen is in training for her job, and she takes her apprenticeship seriously. Throughout the stages of her training, as she has grown in confidence in her ability to cope, she has sensibly concentrated on what she knows best – the children. On her first solo appointment she had them in mind. Her job was simple, but still frightening for a first-timer – a matter of switching on the Christmas lights in Oxford Street the winter after her marriage and making a short speech. 'I know these lights give a great deal of pleasure to countless people in the weeks leading up to 25 December – particularly to families who bring their children to see them,' she said. And in the early days of her first pregnancy, when morning sickness was affecting her badly, she struggled on to several public engagements because, she explained, she mustn't disappoint the children.

Her first public engagement after morning sickness had died down was an unglamorous, if much enjoyed, trip to a school in Brixton, where the Prince of Wales bought her a tin of baked beans for 10 pence and a mango at the school's fair. Her last engagement, in May, at eight months pregnant, was to open the Albany Centre in Deptford, another of London's less wealthy parts. Here she combined both her interests with a tour of the crèche and a chat to the children, after which she looked in on the pensioners' bingo session.

The arrival of Prince William added a whole new dimension to public interest in the couple. Children identified the Prince with their own small brothers and sisters, and asked relentless questions about him on walkabouts, and thrust toys as well as bouquets into the Princess' arms, so that policewomen following Diana were quite laden down with teddy bears. 'The Prince became a symbol for his generation,' said Mr Ian Barnett, after he wrote a celebratory lullaby to welcome him. The song was recorded, appropriately, by a chorus of children between 10 and 12 and an orchestra of pupils under 18, with music by Professor Cyril Lloyd of the Royal Academy of Music – a Welshman, of course. The old people Diana chatted to identified him with their grandchildren. 'Give him a big kiss from me,' said 73-year-old Marie Segal when the Princess visited an old folks' home in Wandsworth and interrupted her in the middle of making apple strudel.

It was not all fun for the Princess after William was born. A combination of exhaustion from the birth and its aftermath and the strain of realizing the kind of pressures involved in the life she had married into, left her astoundingly thin, and some thought unhappy. Rumours and

Left: Diana chats to sympathetic mothers during her visit to Brixton, London, to open a fair at the Dick Sheppard School. This was during her first pregnancy.

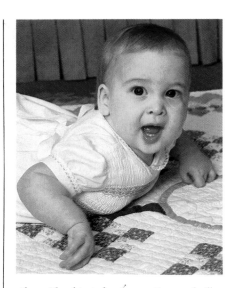

Above: The object of many questions and still more gifts on his mother's walkabouts – Prince William, practising hard for his Australian crawlabout.

stories in the press about her did little to help. The slightest slip, even in answering fan letters from children, was jumped on. When her lady-in-waiting, Hazel West, replied to two Northern Ireland schoolgirls, she forgot her geography and addressed the letter to the 'Republic of Northern Ireland' – a mistake the girls, proud of being part of the United Kingdom and having their own Princess, were quick to tell to the papers. Her inexperience did not excuse her in the eyes of her critics. The demands of her royal job became more obvious. Demonstrations were something the Princess had come across early – on her first visit to Wales she had encountered one, and reacted typically by stopping right in front of the banners to talk to the children who had slipped through the ranks of the protestors. She can always deal with people face to face, but snide critisicm in the papers of such trivial matters as looking too thin, slipping into her seat late for the Royal British Legion Festival of Remembrance on her official visits at the Royal Albert Hall, and seeming less than cheerful was harder to accept.

Diana did deal with it, in her usual fashion, by submerging herself in her work. As soon as she could leave William for long enough, by winter 1982, she was seen out and about on her own. In one period in December she carried out more engagements than any other member of the Royal Family, and without the support of her husband. Somehow, she found the confidence to write to playgroups she wanted to see, to ask if they wanted a visit. That is a tradition she has continued ever since; several institutions have been surprised to find a letter from her office dropping through the door. In hospitals she sat on each bed in the wards she toured, talking in her low voice to every patient. And the children she sat with on the floor in Cirencester, Wandsworth and Birmingham reacted to her as ever, without criticism, and with love.

The children love Diana for herself, and their response must have helped at a time when it appeared the press had only loved her for her pretty face. By now, no doubt, the Princess of Wales is philosophical about the fact that a new pair of seamed tights will be given far more attention and publicity than a visit to a home for handicapped children. At first, as she herself admits, she took remarks in the papers about her to heart. But in time her hard work was noted, and she gained respect when, on a solo visit to Glasgow to open a new kidney unit at the Royal Hospital for Sick Children, she refused to be deterred by the explosion of a letter bomb protesting against her presence and, satisfied that no one had been hurt, carried on without a further thought. That Glasgow visit, which gave Diana a chance to talk to young patients in a field of health where her knowledge is growing, and which included tea with the McAllen family, was typical of the sort of schedule Diana opts for. It suggests a mind that is looking behind the prosperous front civic authorities usually like to present to visiting royalty. And it gives us a very different view of the 'shopaholic Princess', constantly featured by gossip columnists, exploring Sloane Street boutiques.

Diana's job demands that she always looks her best, but it took a child to point out that there was more to her appearance than just clothes, and that her radiance for him did not hide the strain she was under. In the summer Diana found five-year-old James Dove, an ex-pupil from the

Right: In an Arabian's dream of sapphires and diamonds, the Princess of Wales looks wistful at an evening event in Brisbane.

Above: A whole ballet troupe is admired by the Princess who adored ballet when she was a child. A moment on the New Zealand tour.

Young England kindergarten, waiting to greet her in the handshake line-up at the Royal Hospital in Chelsea. 'Jumbo', as she knew him, was not deceived by her cheerful grin and warm greeting. 'She's lovely,' he said perceptively later, 'but she's thin.'

Nevertheless, the thin Princess was beginning to warm to her job. She had discovered the worst and the best of being a full-time member of the family firm and, as in all employment, the initial period was the most taxing. By the time the announcement of her second child was made she had begun to assemble people of her own choosing in her office, rather than rely on those picked for her by The Queen or Prince Charles. Lieutenant-Commander Eberle was one of these, a quiet, modest man who had been in the Falklands campaign and was personally interviewed by the Princess before being taken on as her equerry. Charming, unpretentious, young, he seems to work very easily with the Princess of Wales. With his help she has gained enough confidence to initiate the visits that interest her, make sure that the presents she receives are not too ostentatious, and that the people she talks to are warned not to raise topics that embarrass her – such as her own surprising popularity. The system, she has found, can be made to dance to her own tune. In the same way, she has learned to master the press. From her comments to children and mothers in the crowd on her second visit to Wales after William's birth, it was obvious that Diana had discovered the use to which she could put informal announcements. Princess Michael had been quoted as saying that William had 'red tufts all over his head', and Diana was able to put the record straight by repeatedly informing the

Above: The sight that greets Diana on every tour, and will continue to do so all her life: a line of expectant small faces – and those flags.

crowds at Aberdovey that 'he has the most wonderful mass of blonde hair'. She stopped by another baby William to say firmly how healthy her baby was: 'bigger every day'. Diana was evidently beginning to find that she could influence what was reported in the newspapers if she went about things in the right way.

She has got used to the photographers too. No longer does she duck out of sight, as she did on her first skiing holiday with Charles, and provoke journalists into helicopter sieges. She can smile for the photo sessions she understands are necessary for her work. And in her dealings with the public, she can confidently confess to groups of mothers that she has not felt well from day one of her second pregnancy, and share with them her private hopes that her new baby will be a girl, without feeling her privacy has been left shredded.

It is a confidence which has been hard won. 'We noticed that where she was holding her handbag her nails were bitten and her knuckles were white – she was clenching them,' said an observant young trainee secretary, Elaine Hamilton-Bruce, after Diana's visit to Glastonbury in April to a youth employment centre. 'So she was probably as nervous as us. Although she didn't show it.'

Diana has changed. The shy Princess had learned to do her job better – and will no doubt continue to do it better still. But the rapture with which she is received has not changed over the years since the wedding. And her affection for the children of the land looks like being one of those rare love affairs which can confidently be predicted to last for ever. Happily ever after.

CHAPTER THREE

We Love Our Princess!

Diana is captivated by children – and they are entranced by her. To them she is a fairytale princess come to life, a magical being who is happy, beautiful and good. Children tend to idealize all the Royal Family and their interest in them is intense. Over half the letters The Queen gets are from children. Though they are bowled over by crowns and thrones and palaces, they are also immensely curious about the practical aspects of royal life.

Unlike their parents, they aren't obsessed with gossip or speculation; they show not a flicker of interest in scandal. The kind of things they want to know are what The Queen carries in her capacious handbags, and what the Princess of Wales has for breakfast. Does Prince William keep a hamster? How many rooms are there in the house at Highgrove and does Diana ever get lost wandering through them? How many times does she polish her tiara, and how many dresses has Diana got in her wardrobe?

They come up with the most original questions, which make it obvious that the Royal Family plays an important role in the life of their dreams and imagination. They want to know whether the Princess has a robot to clean her socks and whether, when The Queen sneezes, a special handkerchief, embroidered with the initials E.R., descends on a

Right: (Dale, age 7.) Children do count the differences between the Princess of Wales and the other members of the Royal Family. They sense she has a strong character and will not quite fit into the given mould. They approve when she carries Prince William around with her on her travels and sympathize when she is worried about her husband falling off his horse.

PriNceSS Diana DOES Not like animals as much as the others but I DonT think it matters.

Above: (Sarah, age 9.) It is said that The Queen likes horses and dogs so much because horses and dogs don't realize she is royal. Until recently, the Princess of Wales wasn't royal so she never had to worry whether friends and acquaintances liked her for herself or for her position.

Not being sporty doesn't go against the Princess. In fact, children seem to warm to her for chatting with friends rather than taking an active part in outdoor events.

wire from the ceiling so that she doesn't have to reach for her own. One ingenious mind even devised an electric dress, that works like an electric blanket, keeping the royal ladies warm on cold days and also charging their diamonds to make them flash more brightly.

What – and how much – the Royals eat is intensely interesting to children. They were fascinated to learn that the Princess of Wales likes baked beans and that her favourite sweets are winegums. Children lining the route of a walkabout will often hold a packet of winegums out to the Princess, and sometimes she will accept one. Royal eating habits of the past also fascinate them. Their saliva glands work overtime trying to imagine a surfeit of lampreys and they fantasize about roast peacock or swan with their fried egg and chips.

Every child who has a pet wants to know about the royal animals. They want to know things like the names and ages of the dogs and horses, and whether The Queen's corgis sleep in a fur-lined kennel. Do they eat dog food from the shop, or does their mistress feed them special titbits from the royal table on a gold platter? Why doesn't The Queen like cats? Can Princess Anne's horses talk? The blue budgerigars that live wild at Windsor Castle have them bemused. Why don't they fly away? Perhaps, just like the bluebirds in Walt Disney's film of Cinderella, they helped tie the bows on the Princess of Wales' wedding gown.

Though children love The Queen, they tend to see her as a rather remote figure, and be overawed by her formality. 'She would tell me off if I was naughty,' said one child. 'She's always being strict with Andrew,

Right: (Lucie, age 6.) All princesses live in castles and have pretty hair and pretty clothes . . . and the sun is always shining. Even children as young as six years seem to sense the stability of the Royal Family and its newest Princess. Below: (Toby, age 6.) A portrait of Prince William. Young children tend to believe that the perfect couple have the perfect baby and treat him perfectly. They cannot imagine that Prince Charles would ever get in a temper if the baby Prince cried at night.

and she even gets cross with Philip – you can tell by the way she looks at him.'

If The Queen is thought to do the reprimanding, Diana is *known* to do the cuddling and hugging and kissing better. 'I wish she was my mummy,' more than one child has said, and without embarrassing its own mother. Because of Diana's obvious maternal feelings, children tend to think of Prince William as a baby brother. They want to know if he can talk, swim, write his own name or even ride a horse. The child of a magical princess is endowed with magical powers at a very early age. They want to know how many brothers and sisters William will have, and what they will be called. Children like exotic names and approve of Princess Anne's choice of Zara for her daughter.

William's home life is another topic of intense interest. What colour is his nursery? Does he have a picture of E.T. on his wall? What time does he have to go to bed? Does Princess Diana smack him when he's naughty? Does he have to call his granny Queen?

They are equally curious about the Royals of the past. They store up titbits of information such as the fact that Edward VI wrote a hundred essays in Latin and Greek before the age of 10, and that Edward VII's dog had inscribed on his collar: 'I am Caesar, the King's dog.' When the King died, Caesar followed the coffin in front of the German Emperor.

They are fascinated to find out that Prince Charles walked round the Palace for days before his Investiture wearing his crown, to get used to the weight of it, and that the planes of The Queen's flight travel in special air space called 'purple airways'. Princess Margaret holds a particular place in infant hearts because she grew five different types of potato in her garden as a child, and they feel comforted to know that when Diana was sent to an expensive finishing school in Switzerland, she had to come home after only six weeks because she missed her family so much.

As always, the young are delighted by records. They like to know that The Queen's wedding dress had more pearls sewn on it than any other – 10,000 – and that the Duke of Clarence, son of George III, was the most rejected royal suitor – he was turned down 13 times. The record for royal handshakes is 1547 in one hour 50 minutes at a reception in Washington; and the longest hair belonged to Katherine of Aragon – it was said to fall almost to her feet. The fattest king was Henry VIII, and of course he also had the most wives.

They like to know when something goes wrong in the royal household. Edward VII's coronation had to be postponed when he fell ill with appendicitis, and the magnificent banquet that had already been prepared had to be given away. Only the plovers' eggs and caviare were kept on ice, and the jellies were melted down and stored in champagne bottles. Prince Charles brings a smile to young faces when he falls off his polo pony, because it proves that even royalty isn't perfect.

On the whole, children are fervent supporters of the monarchy. 'I think royal weddings are more fun than James Bond films,' said an American child. There are a few young voices of dissent: 'The Queen has so much money she has to eat pound note sandwiches to get rid of it.' And: 'The Queen sits at home all day counting her money. She never gives any of it away.'

Above: (Evagoras, age 6.) Diana's looks, her hair, her clothes and her hats cause a great deal of admiration from children. They ask as many questions about her wardrobe as they do about what Prince Willliam eats for tea.
Right: (Lynne, age 9.) Children always think that princes and princesses should be really royal with sparkling diamonds, gorgeous clothes, grand carriages, extravagant food . . . and lots of names.

I always like Royal Babies they have so many names.

Right: (Anna, age 11.) Answers to these stock questions are usually . . . 'Yes, someday, but not yet,' and 'Not until she has had more fun.' Children don't like change very much and would quite like The Queen to go on ruling for ever, 'like Queen Victoria'. Unlike Prime Ministers and Presidents who come and go, they feel reassured by the continuity of the monarchy.
Left: (Johanna, age 7.) A romantic vision of the lovely Princess in a beautiful ballgown. The heart-shaped mouth is a warm expression of the love and affection for Diana and the genuine care she so obviously shows for others.

Do you want to be queen?

But most children, and especially those who come from poorer households tell a very different story. 'Princess Diana has to spend so much money on air fares that she can only afford to live on cottage cheese. That's why she's so thin,' explained one little girl. 'I think The Queen ought to have more crowns,' said another. And: 'Diana has to wear the same old clothes twice. She must get so bored.' A 10-year-old revealed: 'When she was Lady Diana the ink in her pen came out silver; now it comes out gold. That's only right for a princess.'

Children, especially the poorer children, do not begrudge the Royal Family its money. They think that palaces and servants, crowns and gold coaches are necessary to the job of being royal, and that the Royals work so hard, they deserve them. But if the Royal Family are symbols of grandeur and glamour, they also represent stability and the warmth of firm family life.

Children dream of walking hand-in-hand with Diana; they dream of playing with Prince William, and being given a ride on the shoulders of Prince Charles. In other words, the Royal Family has almost as important a place in childish hearts as the child's own – it is an extension of the child's family, and one that is without problems, without pain. For children there will always be a place for the fairy tale of royalty, and especially for the Princess they have made their own.

CHAPTER FOUR

Children in Need

Red tartan skirts spread out on the floor, the Princess of Wales is reading aloud from 'The Tiger Who Came to Tea' to a group of attentive toddlers. She has admired their paste sandwiches, refused the offer of adult coffee but accepted one to a juvenile tea in the corner of the playroom with a toy teapot, and she is about to blow soap bubbles and give piggyback rides to all takers.

It is an official royal visit. The press has gone and Diana is making herself at home with the children at the Lewis Lane Playgroup, ten miles from Highgrove, which she herself asked to come and see in action. 'Her Royal Highness fitted into the playgroup so well that we wished we had her on our rota,' commented the Supervisor, Shirley Jones, afterwards. 'I especially admired the way she divided her attention between groups of children. She must have enjoyed herself, for she stayed more than twice as long as planned.'

Diana no doubt enjoyed herself, but she was also working – in the august capacity of Patron of the Pre-school Playgroups Association, one of several charities which she formally became involved in after her marriage. To the public it sounds like a highly suitable, untaxing kind of position in which a nice girl – albeit a Sloane Ranger – can have a pleasant time playing with small children.

But there is rather more to Diana's involvement, and much more to the Pre-School Playgroups Association, than that. For this particular charity, in which Diana so clearly finds herself very much at home, has a set of ideals and aims which tally very closely with the ideas she and Charles apparently hold about the importance of the family, and the importance, in particular, of parental involvement in the education of a child. Officially founded in 1961 as an educational charity for the under fives, it opposes the provision of state nursery schools where parents have taken the responsibility of running them themselves.

Half a million children have playgroups provided for them under the charity. Self-reliance and involvement by their parents is very much encouraged, and many playgroups are organized, equipped and paid for by the Association. In a period when families are so much smaller than they used to be, when so many single parents are isolated in their attempts to give their children a normal upbringing, and so many couples are separated from the relatives and grandparents who would, a century or even half a century ago, have provided natural support, the Pre-school Playgroups Association believes it is providing an essential service. Parents learn, they say, as much from it as the children, by swopping experiences and knowledge with other parents. It is – and Prince Charles would particularly approve of this – an anti-bureaucratic organization with a strong emphasis on the need for parental authority.

'A community playgroup is one in which the parents of the children are responsible for all aspects of the running of the group.' says its manifesto for the eighties. 'In this way it reflects the family structure and

Previous pages: Princess of Wales or Pied Piper? Diana takes the lead in exploring the Charlie Chaplin Playground for handicapped children in Kennington, London.

becomes an extension of it. The benefits are twofold: parents gain confidence from working with their own and others' children and with groups of adults; children benefit from understanding – and we believe that they are sharply aware of the fact – that their parents, who in their eyes represent authority, are recognized by everyone concerned as being indeed in authority.'

With her own children to educate and bring up, these are matters in which the Princess of Wales takes a close interest. Those who have talked to her on the subject say she has read widely on child care. As a working mother herself, enabled by a full-time nanny and other helpers to go about her official duties, she understands how much nursery provision is needed if young mothers are to have a real choice in whether or not to combine work out of the home with the job of rearing children.

Since Diana became Princess of Wales she has made a sustained effort to educate herself about the problems of which she has no experience. In 1982, six months after William's birth, she specially requested a meeting with young mothers at the Hearsay Centre in Catford, set up to help young people with advice on jobs and housing, and supported at the time by the Royal Jubilee Trust, headed by Prince Charles, with about £8,000 a year. 'Some of those she talked to are on the dole and others told her what low wages they had to manage on,' said Mr Harold Marchant, chairman of Youth Aid. 'She was particularly concerned about mothers with small children. She was very clued up about a lot of the problems they face, but I think they told her about some she didn't know.' One girl commented, 'She was very sympathetic and seemed genuinely surprised about what we were facing.'

At around the same time, the Princess, on a quest to learn more about the official view of child care from the headquarters of the Department of Health and Social Security, walked past a bunch of friendly pickets at the Elephant and Castle, protesting about undermanning in the Civil Service. 'We don't mind the Princess coming,' said one picket. 'She is here doing charity work.'

The DHSS has an involvement with the Pre-school Playgroups Association, vetting and approving each playgroup set up. The Association stalwartly asserts, however, that it has as much to teach officialdom as it has to learn from it. Evidence of its influence on official thinking may be seen in a DHSS booklet 'The Family in Society', which suggests that parental involvement in pre-school education can sometimes stop the downward slide of deprived children in primary education.

When the Princess of Wales is seen cheerfully helping sailor-suited children make Mother's Day cards in pasta, blithely ignoring the sticky mess, or showing a four-year-old at the Bovey Tracey playgroup how to stick a self-adhesive 'brick' rather askew on to a picture of a house, in order to launch the appeal for £400,000 to spread her charity's aims further, she is doing more than playing the pretty princess. She is well aware that play is education, too.

It is appropriate that the Princess should have chosen this charity as one of the first to become Patron of, and one in which she has learnt what her role means, and made some of her earliest nervous official

Above: The sight of Diana hand in hand with a small child is quite a familiar one on her many visits to playgrounds and homes.

speeches. For another effect that organization of the playgroups has, of which the Association is particularly proud, is that it gives many new mothers the first opportunity to win confidence in administration and in public speaking – on the platform of the annual, and very popular, AGM.

What the Princess of Wales' role is in the charities she has taken on, is very largely what she makes of it. Patronage offers opportunity. At the least, the royal name on the notepaper, and the occasional visit, gives a charity extra weight, and perhaps a little extra publicity. At the best, well-demonstrated by Princess Anne in her involvement with the Save the Children Fund, a royal patron can provide encouragement, well-educated interest, considered criticism, many thousands of pounds' worth of invaluable press coverage, more thousands of pounds' worth of boost to fund-raising, a constant boost to the morale of the volunteers who meet her at both glamorous and everyday functions, and a representative able to put forward the charity's case at the highest possible levels nationally and, often, internationally. It has taken Princess Anne years to build up the necessary expertise and knowledge to fulfil her role in the Save the Children Fund as well as she does now, but it looks as though Diana, guided by her husband, who probably spends a third of his working time on his Trusts and on charity work, has made a committed beginning in her own area of children's interests.

The role of Patron in a charity also provides a valuable opportunity to learn. Not only is there the usual 'homework' before all royal visits to be carried out – a study of the history and aims of the organization, the people involved in it, and so forth – but there is a constantly developing fund of information gained from talking to the ordinary people as well as the various experts connected with each charity.

Above left: Glamorous evening occasions, like the fashion show Diana attended in this stunning dress by Bruce Oldfield, are very frequently for the serious purpose of raising funds for charities.
Above right: A small child catches Diana's attention on a visit to the Lisson Grove Health Centre, London.

The Pre-school Playgroups Association is looking at ways in which their system can best be used in areas of high unemployment, little money, and, often, with a high teenage crime rate. Prince Charles has been closely involved in the struggle to find practical solutions to the problems of young people, in his work with the Prince's Trust (his own personal charity, which gives grants to individuals – especially those who have been in some minor trouble with the juvenile courts – who put forward worthwhile schemes). He has quite obviously been encouraging his wife to look at similar problems as they affect very young children. One inner city area with which Diana has become closely associated is Deptford, in south London. She is Patron of the Albany Centre there – and she visited it, with its special nursery, as her last public appointment before the birth of Prince William.

Her continuing involvement with the special difficulties children in poor areas face, in particular children of ethnic minorities, has often been demonstrated since. In October 1983 Diana was in Brixton, doing a quick calypso with four-year-old Njoki Kariuki, to a Caribbean-style song which went 'Di long time gal – I never see you'. Again, it was on a visit to a centre with aims after her own heart – to open the West Indian Parents' Family Centre, founded to strengthen family relationships. Play went on around the Princess, with excited children scooting past, as

Diana discussed the work the centre was committed to with its director, Mrs Gloria Cameron.

On her first visit to the West Midlands in her role as Princess, Diana made sure she visited another centre dedicated to giving children a sense of security and pride in their traditions – the ethnic cultural centre in Handsworth – where she smilingly watched six girls, barefoot, dancing the Gahu, a Ghanaian dance. Children deprived by their environment, or at a disadvantage because of their parents' problems with the language or an unfamiliar new country, or through pure discrimination, are a real concern of Diana's.

She is also very sincerely devoted to the interests of children deprived by physical and mental handicap, and visits to their playgrounds and homes figure very strongly on her schedules. On this subject she has an expert close at hand – for her gynaecologist, George Pinker, is deeply committed to the cause of helping to understand and to prevent, where possible, the causes for handicap. On the council of Birthright, a charity devoted to raising funds for research into child-bearing, and

Right: Yet another bouquet for Diana as she visits Brixton.

weaknesses in babies which might lead to handicap, he is well placed to guide and inform her. Diana is aware of the sad fact that 36,000 babies who survive birth have some form of handicap. In order to help raise funds, Diana attended a fashion show held by the charity. Princess Alexandra has also been helping to raise funds. Indeed, the Royal Family's interests in charities run so close that it must often form a topic of eager discussion within their homes.

Inspired in part, perhaps, by these high figures, but more by the sad cases in some of the homes she has visited, Diana has thrown herself into preventive medicine, and has become Patron of the National Rubella Council. To encourage young women to become immunised against German Measles, which can cause deafness or blindness to babies if mothers catch it early in pregnancy, she gave a speech in November 1983 to launch a £2 million national campaign. She revealed that she had had to telephone her father, when she first discovered she was pregnant, in order to check whether she was immune or not. Her involvement in the campaign, and her few simple references to her own baby, won more headlines and press coverage in magazines than a thousand government circulars would have done.

Money from the display of her wedding presents – around £85,000, – went at her decision to charities connected with the disabled and sick children. The Charlie Chaplin Adventure Playground for handicapped children in south London, opened with the help of money from the Borough of Lambeth and the Royal Wedding Fund, and visited by the Princess since, was a typical recipient. Ten days after she had visited it she was out with her husband in Liverpool, launching a canal boat to provide trips for handicapped children – the *Pride of Sefton*. The sight of Diana, laughing and joking, playing with and talking to children suffering from handicaps as she did at a Variety Club lunch in Summer 1983, when lots of small clowns and pierrots turned out to have their day brightened by a Princess dressed in brilliant pink, is now so familiar it hardly causes comment. But all the while Diana's understanding of the problems they suffer, and the contribution she may be able to make is growing. There is every sign that she intends to make it an important and useful one, and not remain just a pretty figurehead. On a visit to Carlisle, as Patron of the British Deaf Association, she told the interpreter who helped her chat to deaf people at the headquarters there that she wanted to try to learn sign language. It would undoubtedly be an immense boost for children, like ten-year-old Lisa Thompson who gave her a bouquet on that visit, to see the Princess talking to them in their own language.

The handicap of blindness is another of Diana's special concerns. She is Patron of the Royal School for the Blind at Leatherhead, which she visited in order to open a new extension, specially designed to enable the residents to achieve more independence, more self-confidence, and eventually to ease themselves back into the streets of their towns or their villages once more, on better terms with their disability. By comparing the different approaches and methods of the various organizations she is becoming familiar with, Diana may learn enough to be eventually very valuable to some of her charities.

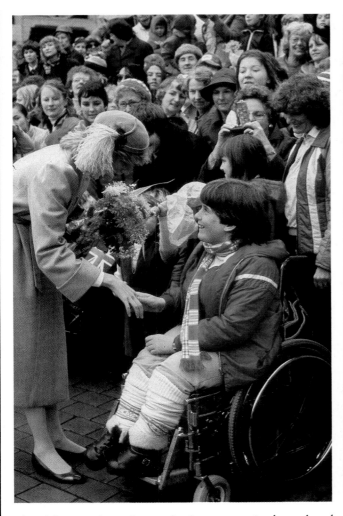

Above left: Diana, during the tour of Wales, takes the hand of a delighted child in a wheelchair.

Above right: A smile that says she's thrilled to be there, at the Sue Ryder Home in Gloucestershire.

At the school she chatted with young and old about her interest – their lives at the school – and their favourite topic, Prince William. It turned out that there was a long tradition of charity work with the disabled in Diana's family – her great-grandfather was one of the founder members of the School for the Blind in 1799. Those who show Diana round on her visits have said repeatedly how curious she is about everything she sees and how eager she is to be informed. At a tour of the Maytrees Home for the Blind in Bristol she spotted a useful aid, speaking clocks, and wanted to know more. 'She was very inquisitive about everything,' said John O'Mahony, the home's rehabilitation officer, 'but particularly the clocks. She asked for a demonstration and we showed her how they worked.'

But it is not enough, as she is well aware, simply to learn herself about the problems the disabled face, and the modern approaches and aids to help overcome them. Her role must be largely one of educating the general public to a better appreciation of the way in which they can help – for it is no use teaching the disabled to integrate back into society if society is not educated to understand and accept their special needs. An imaginative scheme the Princess of Wales lent her particular charisma to was aimed at involving children from schools all over Britain to raise

Above left: Smiling, despite the inclement weather, Diana steps out on a visit to the elderly at Belgrave Lodge, Coventry.
Above right: Waving goodbye after a visit to the Royal Marsden Cancer Hospital, London – a place in which Diana has a very personal interest.

Left: The Patron arrives – Diana at a carol concert for the Malcolm Sargent Fund for Children at the Free Trade Hall, Manchester.

funds for the Royal National Institute for the Blind. Their stories, written for young Prince William, were sponsored by relatives and friends for every twenty words. It exercised their imaginations, made them aware of, and feel involved in, the Royal National Institute for the Blind, and the money was neatly put towards turning other stories and books into braille. Not only was the sponsorship successful – so caught up were children in the excitment of writing for the son of their Princess that they raised over £50,000 – but 14 children achieved brief fame and the ear of the Prince by having their stories published as a book called *Stories for a Prince* – with all royalties, of course, going to the RNIB.

The Princess of Wales, meeting thrilled authors at a reception at the Café Royal, warned them that he was still at the stage when he was more likely to chew than listen. But when all the Princess' children are old enough to understand, they will discover that they too have been drawn into helping other children. Most of the toys, for example, sent to them and given to their parents on walkabouts, or presented by manufacturers in the hope of commercial spin-offs, are passed on to children's charities, hospitals and homes – and the Princess of Wales has by now a very good idea which toys are best appreciated in each of the many places she has visited. 4,200 toys were given when William was born, including useful playgroup props like climbing frames and swings. Some, almost certainly, must be earmarked to help children of her own particular charities – like the Malcolm Sargent Cancer Fund for Children, of which she is also Patron.

Above: Romantically dressed in velvet for another visit to the Royal Marsden, early in Diana's second pregnancy.

The grief which cancer causes when it ravages a young life is something the Princess of Wales has personal experience of. Her own cousin, Conway Seymour, died of leukaemia while she was involved in her love affair with the Prince of Wales, before the engagement was announced. He was only 12 years old when he died, on Christmas day, and his mother, Mrs Alexandra Seymour, pledged herself to raise £200,000 to give the hospital which treated him a vital irradiation machine to help other children combat the disease. Diana and The Queen instantly responded. A private donation was not, however, enough for Diana. In addition she drew public attention to the hospital's work by visiting the Royal Marsden's Fulham section in the winter after William's birth. It was her own idea to call, and it was very successful in publicising the hospital's appeal, as well as providing a welcome lift to the spirits of children such as young Gemma Sanger, being treated for a brain tumour, who gave Diana one of the hospital 'Egbert' mascot figures, designed to cheer up patients. Diana is adept at that, and teased a seven-year-old about her missing tooth. 'It should be 50p', she said, only to be told the rate the fairies in the Marsden worked to was only 10p. 'Because of her visit today many feel a lot better than they did yesterday', said a hospital spokesman as she left. Not content with the one visit, Diana returned eighteen months later to the Sutton branch, where the machine is now enabling doctors to treat children five days a week instead of two.

Above: However did you think of it? Diana gets the low-down on story-telling as she chats to one of the contributors to a book of bedtime stories for William – in aid of the Royal National Institute for the Blind.

At all the hospitals the Princess of Wales visits throughout Britain, she makes a point of asking to meet the Malcolm Sargent Social Worker, if there is one, to talk about the demands of that particular area. Because of her own experience, she can understand better than most the stories of the pressures and strains put on the family of a sick child. She talks to the parents and to the children, giving them both not only a much-needed lift, but the feeling that she genuinely understands. To help raise funds she has so far appeared at a couple of charity concerts – at Manchester, in the Free Trade Hall for a Carol Concert, and at the Royal Albert Hall for the Mountbatten Concert, where some of the Royal Marines who were playing had last entertained her on board Britannia during her honeymoon. Money from the Malcolm Sargent Fund for Children, begun in 1971, goes to alleviate some of the difficulties suffered by children with cancer, leukaemia or Hodgkin's Disease. It bought one small boy, who had lost his sight through cancer, a talking clock because it upset him that he no longer knew the time. It bought a greenhouse for another little boy, suffering at home. More usually it helps pay some of the extra heating costs the parents bear, travel to hospitals, someone extra to look after the other children, or perhaps a last holiday together. Diana's involvement is invaluable in publicising its work.

It is not the only fund-raising for cancer relief which Diana has helped bring into the spotlight. Before her trip to Australia she launched an appeal in Yorkshire, at Garrowby Hall, where the Earl of Halifax, her

Above: Diana, Patron of the National Children's Orchestra, makes her first visit to see the young musicians in action – at Wellington College.

host, is Treasurer of the National Society for Cancer Relief, and she chatted to nurses who work with cancer patients. Then she quietly sent a donation to a charity performance of Noel Coward's *Hay Fever* in aid of leukaemia research.

Lesser known diseases have received valuable attention because of the Princess' interest, too. 'Lupus' for example, a rheumatic disease which can be crippling, was given time on radio programmes and space in papers after the Princess visited experts at the rheumatology unit in Hammersmith Hospital, soon after the announcement of her pregnancy. A young woman near her own age, with a nine-month-old baby boy, told her how she'd gone ahead and had a baby despite the risks her doctors warned her of. Diana smiled at another 'miracle baby', Marcus, handing over some flowers, born to a mother who had spent five years in a stretcher and wheelchairs because of the disease.

Her visits to hospitals may occasionally involve a new contact with a group from the Pre-School Playgroups Association. One of the valuable functions of that charity is to help organize playgroups in hospitals for children.

During her visits to hospitals, the Princess may find some young members of another charity organization of which she is Patron – the youth and juniors branch of the Red Cross. It is a job she took over from Princess Alexandra, who has held it since she was only 15 years old, and who was delighted to hand it over to a young Princess again, though she remains Vice-President of the Red Cross. So many members of the Royal

Above left: At the Great Ormond Street Hospital for Sick Children, London – a very lively visit.
Above right: About to view technology in use – the Princess of Wales opened a new Neonatal Intensive Care Unit at University College Hospital in London in 1983.

Family are associated with the society's work that the senior patrons must frequently find themselves in full assembly over the dinner table in Buckingham Palace or Windsor Castle, for The Queen is Patron and President and the Queen Mother Deputy President. Princess Alexandra, who has something of Diana's informal, direct and friendly charm, should provide an ideal guide to the work of the Red Cross Junior branch. Once, before her marriage, she dropped in to the Stepney Group and joined in the evening's work, finishing off by playing the piano to accompany the Junior Red Cross song.

The work of the children in the Red Cross is very much within Diana's own area of interest as she discovered when she called into its head-quarters in February 1984 (picking up a bunch of carnations some children had dropped) to learn more about it from its chairman and the workers, and to listen to plans to celebrate the Diamond Jubilee of the youth movement. Not that she hadn't already been quizzing the children themselves about what they did, when she spotted the Red Cross badges on the shoulders of children lined up against the barriers on her walkabouts. She has talked to them in Cornwall, in Lancashire and in Durham. At Preston Hospital she was surprised to be told by an eleven-year-old that far from being a new member she was a seasoned campaigner, with four years' work to her credit. And, specially invited to a royal garden party to meet her in July, had been a member with twelve years experience, to tell her what she had done: seventeen-year-old Judy Winter from Leicestershire, who worked every week at the Red Cross toy library for handicapped children and cooked every summer for handicapped campers. Diana told Ian Turner, another member, this time from Stoke-on-Trent, and Judy, that though she didn't know anything about First Aid she was willing to learn it. 'She is a lot more charming face to face than she is on screen,' said Judy, quite delighted. 'Eleven people fainted during the heat, including a Beefeater, and she said she wouldn't know what to do if someone fainted. I said I could cope because I have First Aid proficiency and she seemed relieved.'

Helping handicapped children at holiday camps is a part of Red Cross work that Diana is likely to enjoy learning about. Each year one thousand children with handicaps have the time of their lives. She has already seen the Beauty Care Services in action, dedicated to lifting the morale of hospital patients by giving manicures and simple facials. Young members give special help to old people, as Diana once did as a schoolgirl. The Red Cross also provides crèches at hospitals.

In Australia Diana was visiting an area where the Red Cross had been involved, though she might not have realized it at the time. When the bush fires broke out in South Australia, the Red Cross conveyed anxious messages from relatives in England to the Australian Red Cross, so that news could be quickly passed on.

The Red Cross is, of course, an international organization. Part of its work is to help care for children across the world. Though Diana's interests so far have naturally been chiefly concentrated on children in Britain, she has also begun to learn, on visits to the Commonwealth countries of Canada, Australia and New Zealand, a little about children in need outside the United Kingdom. Her sister-in-law, Princess Anne, is particularly well qualified to tell her more about the international problems which exist in poorer Commonwealth countries – and those outside it. In the summer of 1983 Diana was present adding glamour – and funds – to a charity dinner for which guests were charged £100 a head at Hatfield House, organized by the Marchioness of Salisbury in aid of children in Poland. Despite the glitter of the jewels and surroundings, it was an evening in which the practical urgency of the need was never forgotten – especially by the hostess, who had three times driven van loads of goods across to Poland, taking drugs, food and clothing to mothers in desperate straits.

Prince Charles was also present at Hatfield House, for the two of them work very much as a team in their charity work. On one evening Charles will be seen accompanying his wife to a concert in aid of one of her children's charities. On another, she will be at his side adding appeal to an occasion in aid of the Prince's Trust – a pop concert perhaps – to help the young people who are his particular interest; just before William's birth she went with him to Broadlands for an occasion in aid of United World Colleges, Mountbatten's much-loved educational project which is now in Charles' care. Music is a mutual interest, although Diana enjoys all kinds, whereas Charles' preference is for classical. This is the theme of yet another children's educational charity of which Diana is Patron, the National Children's Orchestra.

Dedicated to giving promising young musicians aged between seven to thirteen the chance to develop their talents by playing together in a

Above: A dazzling Diana at the Royal Albert Hall for a charity pop concert in September 1983.

full symphony orchestra (it has nothing to do with the National Youth Orchestra) it is a young charity itself – only born in 1978. Diana's acceptance of the position of Patron suddenly catapulted it into the national news, especially when she visited the orchestra in working session just before Easter in 1984 to talk to the young musicians, and bewail her own inability to read music at sight.

Their hard work – on their Easter courses the children work a six-hour day – is rewarded by improved skill, the fun of learning together with other children and public performances, some of which the Princess will no doubt attend. (Just in case William or the Princess' other children have a musical bent, she has already been presented with some small-sized musical instruments.)

It is exactly this kind of creative activity which has Charles' and Diana's approval, designed to bring out a child's potential and enjoyment of his talents, combining, in other words, both play and work. Involvement with children and with young people, Diana believes, is, in the words of one of the children of the Orchestra, 'a lot of work mixed with a lot of fun'.

Perhaps the key to Charles' and Diana's devotion to the young could be expressed in the words of Abraham Lincoln: 'A child is a person who is going to carry on what you have started. He will assume control of your cities, states and nations. All your books are going to be judged, praised or condemned by him. The fate of humanity is in his hands.'

CHAPTER FIVE

Young Fans Abroad

The Princess of Wales embarked on her first foreign tour in March 1983 and, despite the fact that her destination was the other side of the world, the nine-month-old Prince William went with her. With typical strength of character, Diana was setting a royal precedent as a working mother. When The Queen was only eight months old in 1927, her parents left her at home with her grandmother Queen Mary and sailed to Australia without her. They returned with more than two tons of toys, but nothing could have compensated for their absence. 'Babies,' as Diana has said, 'need a lot of loving.'

Putting her love for her infant son and her recognition of his needs first, Diana took another step away from royal tradition and decided that the two men in her life – first and second in line to the throne – should fly in the same plane. After all, statistics show that accidents are more likely on the road than in the air. The baby's safety on the ground was supervised by Charles' cousin Richard, Duke of Gloucester. As president of the Road Safety Association he was able to advise on carrycot safety straps, which were duly fitted in all the cars William might travel in Down Under.

Neither was Diana deterred by the risk of infection. Babies don't normally finish their state vaccination course until they are in their second year, but she rightly judged that by keeping William away from close public contact – though not out of the public eye – he would be perfectly safe.

Thus it was that in a Boeing 707 equipped with a sky cot, a mountain of disposable nappies and a good supply of Malvern water for mixing dried baby food, the greatest show on earth took to the air. The mundane cargo did not detract from the fact that the Princess was also taking with her a vast and glamorous wardrobe and jewels of inestimable value – on the contrary, the trappings of motherhood were to be her passport to the heart of Australasia.

Diana was still very young – only 21 – to undertake such an important tour, but though it was a gruelling six weeks, the massive adulation of the crowds gave her a new confidence and enabled her to say: 'I am doing my job better now as Princess of Wales than I previously did.' She had obviously learned a lot from her predecessors. The Queen Mother remembered her first year as a Royal leaving her 'absolutely worn out'. She has told Diana: 'Forget yesterday and tomorrow – when you are meeting people, today is the most important day and the person to whom you are talking is the most important person.' If she ever flags, Diana can recall Queen Mary's words to a novice who complained of fatigue: 'Stuff and nonsense, you are a member of the British Royal Family, and *we* are never tired.'

But inevitably Diana's strongest support came from her husband and the presence of her baby son. And while William was with his nanny and the Princess was on duty and learning the ropes, her juvenile support

Diana, the Children's Princess

came from the crowds. No amount of crowd control could stop children running up to Diana to give her flowers and it was this, more than anything else, that made her feel at home half way round the world.

The Royal party's first stop in Australia was at Alice Springs. They appeared on the airport tarmac as a threesome, the presence of Prince William setting the theme for his father's speeches for the next few weeks on the importance of the family and the Commonwealth. The torrential rain and flooding that had threatened to disrupt the royal visit had given way to brilliant sunshine. Floods had wrecked the hotel where the Wales' were to have stayed, so workmen had been called in to put some last-minute royal touches to the Gap Motor Hotel. The chief minister for the Northern Territory was convinced that his guests would not be disappointed. 'I understand their taste is for simple things,' he said. 'They are steak and eggs people.' In 'the Alice' it would not do to be otherwise, for this is Australia at its rawest – drinking is the most popular form of recreation and pomp and pommies are usually looked upon with contempt.

While Diana proceeded to charm even the most Republican section of the population, William was taken back onto the plane by nanny Barbara Barnes for his journey to the family's Australian base at Woomargama. There he stayed in a luxurious stone farmhouse loaned to the couple by millionaire Gordon Darling. William's arrival coincided with the first rainfall in Woomargama in four years, gladdening the hearts of the local farmers, who christened him 'Billy the Kid'. It seemed that rain-bringing was a family talent, for William's grandmother The Queen was at that moment in California, being greeted by the wettest weather in living memory.

In Alice the temperature was in the 90s and while Diana was recovering from jetlag, lying in her bikini by a private pool, she got 'rather sore'. On the first day of their tour the Prince and Princess inspected the flood damage. Then they went on to visit the School of the Air, which gives lessons by radio to over 100 children on remote homesteads within a 600-mile radius of Alice. The Princess was in her element answering the children's questions, all of which had been vetted by Buckingham Palace. The only one the Palace had turned down was about Prince Charles' night attire – did he wear pyjamas, an inquisitive youngster wanted to know. This remained a royal secret, but Diana did reveal that Prince William liked to play with a plastic whale in his bath, though he was 'a bit small', as she tactfully put it, for a bicycle.

After the broadcast Diana and Charles went on their first walkabout and were given a rapturous welcome by 3,000 local children. 'There is one sure way of getting the Princess to stop and talk to you,' said an adult member of the crowd. 'You should be not much more than five and feeling a little lost and bewildered.' Diana paid special attention to the Aborigine children and even astounded them by speaking a few words in their dialect. They in turn delighted the Princess by addressing her as 'mummy' and Charles as 'daddy'. Diana's rapport with the children was instant. One four-year-old grabbed her hand and threatened never to let go – Diana's training as a kindergarten teacher often came to her aid in the face of what could have been awkward over-enthusiasm.

Right: Captivating another toddler at Alice Springs.
Below: Knee-level hysteria amongst the children of Alice, as Charles and Diana crouch down to have a good chat.

Next on the agenda was a pilgrimage to Ayer's Rock, the world's largest monolith 200 miles from Alice in the 'dead heart' of Australia. Like countless other tourists, Charles and Diana went there to climb the rock and take snaps of the sunset, which in a spectacular light show turns the fantastic red sandstone formation from orange to flaming scarlet, to purple and finally to deep black. Though the sunset provided a marvellous display, all eyes were on Diana, who looked deliciously cool in a crisp white dress and flat shoes – a photographer's dream against the sunbaked background.

This is Aborigine country, but here as elsewhere in Australia, the Aborigines forgot for a day the 200 years of bitter wrangling over the land taken from them by white immigrants, and chose not to embarrass the couple with protests. Instead they presented Charles with some fine examples of their carving and gave Diana a badge saying 'I climbed Ayer's Rock'.

More children had turned out to welcome the couple at Tennant Creek in the outback. Some of them had travelled over 500 miles to sing 'I can't spell hippopotamus', which they had been rehearsing for months. Diana kept smiling, but the temperature was 98 degrees and her English rose complexion was beginning to suffer. 'I can't cope with the heat very well,' she admitted to her young fans. Though she had brought a stunning collection of hats with her, she had not worn one of them so far and even her dark glasses, essential against the punishing glare of the Australian sun, were taken off while she talked to the crowds lining her route so they could get a better look at her face.

Not long before the royal visit, bush fires had ravaged vast areas of South Australia and Victoria, and 72 people had lost their lives. Showing typical concern, Charles asked if they might inspect the damage and meet some of the homeless and the firefighters who had rescued them. As they talked to the bereaved of Cockatoo, Victoria, where 46 people had died, Diana carried the Australian flag. Both shook hands with a young volunteer fireman who had been badly injured. After this sad episode, William claimed his mother's attention and the Wales' flew to Woomargama near the Victoria-New South Wales border to join him and relax for a couple of days.

On 23 March the royal pair flew to Canberra for their official welcome from Labour Prime Minister Bob Hawke and his wife. Republican feeling was known to be running high in the capital, and enthusiasm for the heir to the throne was expected to be muted. Though Mr Hawke did not bow as he shook hands with the Prince and Princess, his wife Hazel curtsied to them both. But Diana's lively charm immediately relaxed any tension that might have been in the air, and the Prime Minister was able to put politics behind him for the duration of their stay. He and his wife visibly enjoyed the company of the Prince and Princess – she made him roar with laughter and later he commented on her 'beautiful eyes'.

If the people of Canberra were anti-royal at heart they did not show it. A crowd of 6,000 waited two hours in the Civic Centre for a glimpse of their visitors. Jill Shoebridge, a 30-year-old housewife, held her 15-month baby in her arms, and he was crying in the sun. Diana walked over to speak to her. 'I wish I had a nanny to look after my baby like you

Below: Throughout the Australian tour children waved banners to attract the Princess, here feeling the hot sun at Tennant Creek. Right: The Prince and Princess, whom some Aboriginal children insisted on addressing as 'mummy' and 'daddy', at the sacred spot of Ayer's Rock, at the start of their tour.

Left: Diana hearing first-hand accounts of the bush fires from the children of Stirling in the Adelaide Hills.

Below: It was a trip full of joy as well as sadness. Diana was highly amused by Charles' impetuous dancing style when they took to the floor at a charity ball in Sydney.
Overleaf: Stadiums full of schoolchildren abounded on the tour. Charles and Diana both became expert at fielding bouquets – here at Bunbury, south of Perth.

have,' Jill told her. 'It must be marvellous to go off and relax sometimes.' Princess Diana looked amazed. 'Oh, I'd swap places with you any time,' she said. 'I'd much rather have William with me than leave him behind with his nanny.' Jill felt that Diana had spoken from the heart. 'She didn't look too happy when she said she had to leave William behind . . . I don't envy her her royal lifestyle at all.'

At moments like these Diana gives a rare glimpse of the sadness of a young mother whose work takes her away from the nursery. As Diana's own home life was disrupted from the age of six, when both her mother and her nanny left her, it is inevitable that the small nucleus of her new family should mean everything to her – and that she should want to surround William with the warmth and love that she herself was denied.

On 28 March Diana and Charles arrived in Sydney, totally unprepared, as were the tour organizers, for the frenzied enthusiasm that greeted them. That most sophisticated of cities went wild, many of its inhabitants camping overnight on the pavements to ensure a sighting of the Princess. There were not enough barriers or police to contain the crowd, and in the stampede small children were crushed and separated from their parents as officials looked on helplessly. 'It was almost mass hysteria,' said an assistant police commissioner. 'This was adoration.' The couple took refuge at a banquet where the table was adorned with a koala bear fashioned in ice, a state crest made of butter and – the *pièce de résistance* – two flamingoes fashioned out of lard. Diana was visibly moved as her husband thanked the people for the way they had taken his wife to their hearts and 'enveloped her in warmth and affection'.

Wherever he and Diana went, Charles was as always the perfect gentleman, conceding on every possible occasion that it was her the crowds had turned out for and not him. When he went solo on walkabouts he had to apologize constantly for his wife's absence, especially to disappointed children. 'Where's Lady Diana then?' asked one crestfallen little soul. 'It's not fair, is it,' joked Charles. 'You'd better ask for your money back.' And on another occasion: 'I'm sorry about that. You'll have to put up with me.'

The royal couple spent Easter quietly at Woomargama with William, overwhelmed by thousands of chocolate Easter eggs, boomerangs and koala bears. On Easter Sunday they attended church and it surprised no-one that the congregation was the largest for years, with a 200-strong crowd standing outside the church listening to the service on loudspeakers.

Tasmania, Adelaide, Port Pirie and Renmark followed in quick succession, and everywhere the children came first. In Port Pirie Charles received a kiss on the cheek from a 16-year-old trophy winner ('more fun than winning the trophy,' she said), while Diana, as usual, catered for the younger end of the market. But not all her encounters with children followed the expected pattern. In Renmark a two-year-old boy demanded the return of a posy his mother had persuaded him to give the Princess, and Diana complied with a laugh. On a walkabout in South Australia she patted a tousled mite on the head and asked him why he was not at school. 'I was sent home, miss,' the little chap replied, 'because I've got head lice.'

The royal couple received the same tumultuous welcome in Perth that had greeted them in Sydney. As they travelled round the city in a motorcade, children who could not hand the Princess their flowers personally flung them into the royal car. Diana fielded one bouquet in mid-air, winning herself the kind of ovation Australians normally reserve for their cricketers.

After Melbourne and Brisbane it was off to New Zealand. Here in this most royalist of Commonwealth countries the tour was somewhat marred by Maori protesters, who made their point in the struggle for land rights by letting off stink bombs and pouring quick-set cement into lavatories. One man was arrested for lifting his grass skirt and presenting the couple with a good view of his bottom.

Two other aspects of this part of the tour cast a cloud. The British photographers came up against unwelcome red tape from the New Zealand authorities and the New Zealand Premier, Robert Muldoon, used the presence of the royal couple for his own ends – he addressed the crowds who had turned out to see them as if they had gathered for a political rally. But these irritations paled to insignificance in the light of the New Zealander's wild enthusiasm for Diana and Charles. At their farewell banquet in Auckland the Prince summed up: 'My wife has proved, apart from anything else, that she is as good as the next woman

Below: A young New Zealander meets the Princess at Lower Hutt, near Wellington.

at the art of hongi-ing (the New Zealand nose-rub greeting). Both our noses will carry the memory of this particular tour.' He added that the Princess, who was suffering a little from a sore nose after so much hongi-ing, had been delighted with the Maori singing and dancing she had witnessed.

But undoubtedly the highlight of the New Zealand visit was Prince William's photocall on the lawns at Government House. As the whole world waited, the royal babe was set down on a floral rug for his first formal crawlabout. As 60 cameras whirred, Diana's son obediently crawled, stood on his toes (with the aid of his mother), gurgled and said something that sounded remarkably like 'Dada'. 'Who's a little superstar then?' Diana whispered to him in obvious pleasure.

When the visit was over, the *Melbourne Herald*, Australia's bestselling evening newspaper, said it all with a cartoon map of the country superimposed with a heart inscribed 'Princess Diana'. The caption read 'A permanent imprint'. Diana-mania had swept the continent. Men had pushed forward in the crowds to kiss her hand, and £45 tickets for the ball she attended in Sydney had sold on the black market for as much as £1,800. But it was not Diana's glamour, but the love of a young mother for her child that had finally captured the heart of Australasia and its children.

Below left: A toy fire engine for Prince William from firemen at Auckland. William, on the plane home, tactfully demanded a kiwi toy in lieu of his cuddly koala.
Below right: By the end of the tour Diana had learnt plenty about Maori customs at first hand – including the art of nose rubbing.

Left: The Superstar who was the subject of much curiosity from children in Australia and New Zealand – Prince William, first finding his own two feet on New Zealand soil.

Sadly, William was left behind on the royal visit to Canada. 'Wills', the nickname his father is known to use, though he has said publicly that William's name would never be abbreviated, was sorely missed, not least because he celebrated his first birthday while his parents were away. Diana and Charles spoke to their son on the phone and told the press that they had left him several small presents in the nursery, though the big present would have to wait until their return. What would it be? They were vague, except that it would have to be unbreakable.

While the one-year-old received thousands of cards and presents from all over the world, his mother was earning herself glowing praise from Canadian journalists despite a few controversial incidents. During a press reception aboard the Royal Yacht *Britannia*, Diana had revealed off the record that she was still suffering from a childlike – and completely understandable – vulnerability. 'When the wolf pack-like British tabloid press . . . write something horrible I get a horrible feeling right here [pointing to her chest], and I don't want to go outside.' She also confessed: 'It will probably take five or ten years for me to get used to it.' One of the journalists present caused a massive row by breaking the confidence observed round the world on such occasions and

Right: The children of Ottawa had also learnt that banners attracted Diana by the time she arrived there for her Canadian tour.

publishing every word Diana had said. The Nova Scotian *Daily News* has now been banned from any future press receptions given by members of the Royal Family.

In another incident, Victor Chapman, Diana's press secretary, had accused a tv crew of placing a microphone too close to the Princess' leg while she was visiting a national park in Newfoundland. Then there was an over-enthusiastic speech by the Premier of New Brunswick, Mr Richard Hatfield, in which he referred mysteriously to 'lies', proposed a toast to 'love the Prince and Princess of Wales', and capped it all by saying: 'Let the flame burn to warm hope, to extinguish cynicism and despair, to heat the soul that remains and remembers.' Later Mr Hatfield confessed that he had been drunk – but not on alcohol. 'Yes, of course I was drunk. Drunk on her charm and beauty.' Despite these hiccups, the 17-day visit to Canada was a terrific success. *Maclean's Magazine* spoke of Charles and Diana as the most glamorous royal couple in the world and added: 'The Royal Family's grip on the heartstrings of the nation is undiminished.' And a nationally syndicated columnist pointed out why – Diana and Charles were a hit because of 'the way this royal visit got to the young people, the supposed unreachables who were going to let the monarchy fade away.' As he rightfully stressed, it is Diana's endless and

Below: The fairytale Princess come to life – Diana dressed in blue and silver and the Spencer tiara in New Brunswick.

Above: Prince Charles offers an encouraging hand to Diana in Saint John, New Brunswick.

very special appeal to the young that will take the monarchy into the 21st century on a wave of public love and approval.

In Newfoundland the Princess had a soul-searching conversation with Premier Brian Peckford, which highlighted one of the reasons for her compatibility with children. Forced so early into the public eye, and with none of the royal training her husband has had, Diana has sometimes felt like a child herself in a sophisticated adult world. Days before her 22nd birthday – which was celebrated with a banquet, while a crowd of 62,000 sang 'Happy Birthday to You', and a private champagne party with Charles on the plane home – the Princess admitted to Mr Peckford that she had had to grow up quickly to cope with the strain of being the future Queen of Britain and the Commonwealth and constantly at the centre of world attention. 'I am finding it very difficult to cope with the pressures of being the Princess of Wales, but I am learning to cope with it. I have learned a lot in the last few months . . . and I feel I am doing my job better now than I was before. I have matured a lot recently and got used to coping with things.'

Mr Peckford, like the rest of Canada, fell under Diana's spell. He was particularly moved by her concern for children. 'She almost cried when she was told that a little boy who had presented her with a bouquet was blind. She hadn't realised at the time and was deeply touched when someone told her.'

Diana appeared embarrassed, said Mr Peckford, at Prince Charles' public reference to the fact that they wanted a large family, but 'The way I assess it is that if he had said something like that in private she would come back with some quip. When there is a crowd and she can't do that, she gets embarrassed – but she is growing up so fast that in a few months she won't be.'

Left: The focus of all eyes at Edmonton, age 22 that day – and still collecting presents for Prince William.

Charles mentioned his hopes for several companions for William three times. At a youth festival in St John, Newfoundland, he told an audience of 5,000 children that he wished to enlarge his family and Diana blushed and muttered under her breath: 'How embarrassing'. Charles went on to say: 'My wife deserves a medal for the first one.' Just before he and Diana had left for their Canadian tour, the Prince told a conference at the London Business Studies Centre: 'The royal breeding programme is now firmly underway.' Mr Peckford and his wife told the Princess how much they wanted a son of their own, and her parting remark was: 'Make sure now that there is another male in the family.'

As for her own son, as soon as Diana arrived in Canada she confided to two Halifax grandmothers: 'I miss William very much. I'm very sorry we couldn't bring him this time – but we will next time.' Charles spoke about how William and his brothers and sisters would be raised. 'I would like to bring up our children to be well mannered, to think of other people, to put themselves in other people's positions,' he said. 'If they are not very bright or very qualified, at least if they have reasonable manners I believe they will go further in life.'

Many of Diana's fans dissolved into tears after meeting her. 'You hear so much about her, I can't believe she's real,' sobbed one woman. A 17-year-old girl confessed herself 'freaked out', and a young housewife whom Diana had asked 'Is it really summer?' broke down and wept. 'I don't know why I'm crying,' she sobbed. 'I'm so happy.' Men were no less emotional. 'I can't talk,' said a garage mechanic. 'I can't describe how I feel . . . I touched her.' It seemed that the only dry eyes in Canada belonged to the children. Everywhere they greeted Diana with spontaneous enthusiasm. They mobbed her car, they released a skyful of helium-filled balloons, they sang 'God Bless the Prince of Wales' and a folk song, 'Jack was every inch a sailor, four and twenty years a whaler', that had the Princess singing along as loud as the rest. Only in the company of small children does Diana completely lose her shyness and act as she would if no-one, let alone the whole world, was watching. One young boy scout will never forget the moment the Princess of Wales bent down to straighten his tie – the absent-minded gesture of a natural mother.

Even when she's enjoying herself meeting children, Diana's job is exhausting. One of her private staff has said: 'The nervous energy she expends before any official engagement is frightening. She gives everything she has got. Originally, the Princess found it really difficult talking to strangers, particularly with everyone in the room watching her every move. But she has learned to pace herself. This way she can survive better, both physically and psychologically.'

Nevertheless, because of her 100-per-cent commitment, the job still takes its toll. After a day of shaking hands, smiling, listening and saying the right thing hundreds of times over, Diana is 'flaked out – exhausted – shattered – utterly drained. She slumps in a chair and lies there quietly without saying a word.' It is at times like these that privacy means everything to the Princess at the centre of the world's attention – and the Children's Princess wishes for nothing more than to be a Princess for her own children alone.

CHAPTER SIX

Royal Childhood

At the moment the Princess of Wales is the focus of interest in the Royal Family, and partly because of her love of children and her absorption in the role of wife and mother. But she is far from being the only member of the family to hold those traditional values dear. For the Royal Family shows the extended network of relationships still operating in a way which is rarely seen in this age of the nuclear family. The Royals form a vast and growing clan, who are abundantly supportive of each other and rush to the defence of any of their number who comes under criticism from outside. As Lord Snowdon has said, they are 'a circle with a language as private as patois,' whose members can feel relaxed within its bounds as they can never do elsewhere.

On the steps of St George's Chapel, Windsor, at Christmas, a larger group of Royals can now be seen than has been entertained at the castle for years. The Queen, the matriach at the head of the clan rules benignly over a realm of in-laws, cousins, children, godchildren and grandchildren in a way which is beginning to look very reminiscent of the years of Victoria's maturity. As time goes by, some observers have noted, she is even beginning to look a little like her noted ancestress – and she can certainly put to good effect a very familiar freezing glance when confronted with unruly pressmen or a breach of etiquette. But though she is as passionately concerned as Victoria was with keeping the family network together, and looking after its members, she is a far more tolerant, amused, and liberal matriach than her possessive predecessor ever was. She swiftly summons a charming smile when confronted by the children in her care – indeed, it sometimes looks as though only children and the horses she adores so much can produce that spontaneous, natural smile which transforms her face. It was very evident on the day she left the hospital after her first glimpse of her first grandson, Peter Phillips, Princess Anne's child.

Peter Phillips was born when the nucleus of the Royal Family was still quite small, but while Victoria was on the throne, the royal links extended across the world. There were few European monarchs who did not carry some of her blood in their veins. It was hoped in Victoria's day that these extended family links, reinforced by arranged marriages and kept alive by long and intense correspondences, might help to preserve European peace. But that hope finally shattered in 1914 when the Kaiser declared war upon his cousin, George V. Today close friendships between royal families are not expected to smooth international political relations. This was demonstrated at the time of Charles and Diana's wedding when the King of Spain – a highly respected friend of the groom's – did not attend the service because the honeymoon cruise was due to start from Gibraltar, territory to which his country laid claim.

William and his brothers and sisters will find comparatively few thrones left and few reigning relatives, though those in exile still form

Right: The future heir to the throne may have good reason to look perplexed at the amount of public attention he already receives.

part of the royal clan. Ex-King Constantine of Greece, still called King of the Hellenes at the Wedding despite his absence from his throne, is one of William's godfathers, and very much part of the Royal Family's private life. Just before her Canadian tour the Princess of Wales found time to slip into St Mary's, Paddington, to congratulate Queen Anne-Marie, Constantine's wife, on the birth of the couple's fourth child, Princess Theodora, to whom The Queen stood godmother at yet another family christening.

Family christenings are, of course, great occasions for the gathering of the clans, symbolizing as they do the family's continuity. And the Royal Family celebrates them with a ceremony which has long disappeared from the lives of most of their subjects – though perhaps, if the Princess of Wales stars in many more of them, there will be a renewed fashion for formal services with all the dressing up, and the parties afterwards where grandmothers can be seen eagerly swapping family anecdotes.

Few, though, can run to ceremonies on the royal scale. Traditionally these incorporate the gold christening font, designed by Prince Albert, for the use of the Archbishop of Canterbury in the Music Room of Buckingham Palace, and the Honiton lace christening robe first worn by his eldest child. These splendid trappings, like the long list of names royal children are given, underline the significance of the past in the present lives of members of the Family.

Prince Charles emphasized the links between the generations when he chose the 82nd birthday of the Queen Mother for the christening of her great grandson: 4 August 1982. Queen Mary had been photographed holding Charles, her great grandson, in her arms: Victoria was photographed with her great grandson, Mary's eldest, Edward VIII. This time the traditional photograph spanning the years did not impress Prince William by its historic nature; he wailed constantly in the Queen Mother's arms and refused to be comforted until his blushing mother gave him a finger to suck.

When the pictures were published the discussion over whom the new baby resembled was a game shared by the whole nation. So well known are the faces of the Royal Family through the years that royal children find their hereditary characteristics discussed up and down the land with as much familiarity as a village gossiping over the latest addition to its community. Prince William's face was eagerly scrutinized. Some – including Lady Fermoy, his great grandmother on Diana's side – thought he looked like Charles' mother. 'Prince William is growing more like The Queen every day,' she said. But the general opinion was that he was the spitting image of his maternal grandfather. 'I should think about 20 people have told me,' said a proud Earl Spencer.

The christening of a future king may be a special event, but christenings are far from rare at the moment in the Royal Family. Luckily for the children of Diana and Charles, they are right in the middle of a whole new generation of royal babies and of small cousins in every direction. For them it is a piece of good fortune that will protect them both from loneliness and from any tendency to think themselves special. It seems highly unlikely, for example, that Prince William will ever be permitted to pull rank with Princess Anne's daughter, plain Miss Zara Phillips.

Right: The Prince and Princess give their son a steadying hand as he tries out his legs in the garden of Kensington Palace.

Besides Princess Theodora, not too far from Kensington in her parents' home in Hampstead, there are Princess Michael of Kent's children, Lord Frederick Windsor and Lady Gabriella, next door in Kensington Palace and in their country residence near enough to Highgrove in Nether Lypiatt Manor – an excellent place to play, with its tales of ghosts inside, and its pet goats outside. There are the Duchess of Gloucester's children, the Earl of Ulster, Lady Davina Windsor and Lady Rose Windsor; then there are the children of Lady Jane Fellowes in the Barracks at Kensington Palace. Diana's other sister, Lady Sarah McCorquodale, has a daughter, and though she lives on a farm in Lincolnshire, Laura will often join her cousins at Balmoral and Highgrove and visit them in London too. And finally there are the children of Diana's and Charles' close friends, particularly those of Lord and Lady Romsey, who, as part of Earl Mountbatten's family, are so closely linked by blood and friendship to the Royal Family. Lord Romsey is another of William's godfathers: Prince Charles stood godfather to his son, Nicholas Knatchbull, and the Princess of Wales is godmother to their daughter, Alexandra. And Diana's other goddaughters, Lady Edwina Grosvenor, and her sister Lady Tamara, children of the Duke and Duchess of Westminster, are also going to be part of this new generation of playmates. There will be plenty more names to add to the list in the next few years.

Above left: Peter and Zara Phillips and Princess Anne at the Royal Windsor Horse Show. The fourth member of the group is a bodyguard, a feature of their outings that all young royals soon learn distinguishes them from other children.

Above right: Family and friends are often one and the same for members of the Royal Family. The Duke and Duchess of Gloucester's children – the Earl of Ulster, Lady Davina and Lady Rose – will be good companions for the Princess of Wales' children in the future.

These are the children who will, for the next decade and more, be meeting for parties and outings, be found romping in the swimming pool at Buckingham Palace, and inventing their own in-jokes and language to add to the Royal Family's patois and exclude the older members from their secrets. They will soon learn, too, as their parents did, that those secrets can only be told to members of their own circle. The more there are in your peer group in the Royal Family, the better, for such are the pressures of this goldfish-bowl existence that your equals are the only people in whom you can confide. They are the only ones who will understand your special problems; the only ones to whom you may be rude and fight with at times – the only people, in other words, with whom you can be truly yourself. Inside that group, as Prince Edward once pointed out, it is like any other family. Outside it, small royals suddenly have to be unfailingly polite with the eyes of the world upon them.

In these circumstances it is no surprise that the Monarch's clan keeps close together, or that that closeness is marked by a pattern of great family gatherings at Sandringham in the New Year, at Windsor at Christmas, at Balmoral in autumn, when the nurseries of the great castles are full to overflowing and flocks of nannies can be seen taking their charges for their first tastes of that fresh air the adult Royals are so fond of. Prince Charles' nanny used to marvel at the conditions they would cheerfully go out into.

If the setting and the numbers seem Victorian, so will the court etiquette these children will learn from infancy. Even as a small child The Queen was taught to curtsey to her father, George VI. Though the Queen relaxed the custom for Charles and Anne and their brothers and much of the formality between parents and children has disappeared, the manners the young Royals will be taught for state occasions will still be those of the last century. The Queen and Prince Philip do not allow liberties and are well aware of the special danger royal children face of being spoilt by too many attendants and too much attention, but they are nevertheless fond grandparents. And like all grandparents they are happy to take their grandchildren out from under their parents' feet from time to time and have them to themselves – though it must be added that the presence of nannies makes the operation easier. When he was 18 months old William left his parents in peace at Highgrove and went to spend the first part of the New Year with his nanny and all his Christmas toys in Sandringham, where cousins Zara and Peter were already ensconced.

At Sandringham and Balmoral the new generations will be taught the traditional sports of the country gentleman – and lady too, for the Princess of Wales can handle a gun, though she does not care for horses. Two Scottish great-grandmothers will be at hand to help instil in them a knowledge of horses and country pursuits – Ruth, Lady Fermoy, Diana's grandmother, and the Queen Mother herself, her great friend. Both are passionate about steeplechasing – and when the children go over to Birkhall, the Queen Mother's house near Balmoral, they are likely to find themselves equipped with fishing rods, for it was the Queen Mother who taught Prince Charles to fish. With her childlike love of mischief and fun, the Queen Mother is likely to form an ally on all crucial occasions. If grandparents are allowed to spoil children a little, great grandparents are at liberty to go to whatever lengths they please. Even the rigid Queen Mary unbent with little Charles and Anne.

The Queen Mother's other home in Scotland, the charmingly restored Castle of Mey, in its remote setting six miles from John O'Groats,

Below: Prince Charles and his gun dog Harvey return from a fishing expedition. Fishing is a favourite away-from-it-all recreation for the Prince – a passion he shares with the Queen Mother.

and thus far from the reach of normal pressmen and intruders, will form another retreat: one of the few places where royal children can relax completely. Another, not quite as isolated, but almost as secure, will be on the Isle of Seil in Scotland, where their grandmother Mrs Shand Kydd can entertain them on her husband's 1,000-acre hill farm, often the scene of Diana's own school summer holidays. Mrs Shand Kydd intends to play a large part in her grandchildren's lives. She is an energetic woman of character with an occasional touch of unconventionality – a journalist who interviewed her in Australia was astonished to note that she was wearing red ribbons tied round her ankles. So that she is free to spend more time with her growing family, Mrs Shand Kydd has given up the newsagents-cum-sweet shop she once ran in Oban. To her delight, one of her customers once congratulated her on not venturing an opinion on the new Princess of Wales – after all it would not be fitting from a mere shop assistant. The customer added: 'One thing is for certain, she didn't come out of a home like you and I did.' Mrs Shand Kydd does not come out of an average home, but she certainly has a first-hand view of how average people regard royalty, and this will be invaluable to her royal grandchildren. She managed brilliantly to guide her daughter through the difficulties of dealing with the press before her engagement, and she will also well understand how much her grandchildren need to be removed from the pressures of publicity. When they visit her on the sheep and cattle ranch in Australia, at Yass,

Below: Ties of family and friendship are strong in the Royal Family. The Queen Mother is seen here with her close friend and Woman of the Bedchamber – Ruth, Lady Fermoy, who is also Diana's grandmother.

Above: The Earl Spencer after visiting his newborn grandson.
Below: Mrs Shand Kydd at Yass, New South Wales, Australia.

New South Wales, they will be able to enjoy themselves and discover the freedom from formality that Charles so much enjoyed in his time at Geelong School's country outpost, Timbertop. 'In Australia', he has said, 'you are judged on how people see you and feel about you. There are no assumptions. You have to fend for yourself.' This is the kind of self-reliance that Mrs Shand Kydd will encourage in her grandchildren. She will be a good teacher, having been forced herself to develop enormous resilience and strength after her painful divorce from Earl Spencer and loss of the custody of her four children.

The influence of Diana's side of the family on William and his brothers and sisters is likely to be strong. As Earl Spencer has remarked, they have no intention of being swamped. 'Prince William will grow up close to the Spencer side of the family and be influenced by them as much as by the Royals,' he said proudly just before the couple made their visit to Canada. 'I know the Royals can appear to swallow people up when others marry in, and the other family always looks as if it had been pushed out, but that could never happen to us. We can cope with the pressures. We have been brought up with royalty and there is no question of us being pushed out. Diana would not permit it to happen. And she always gets her own way.' Sure enough the figure of William's Spencer grandfather, whose height and facial characteristics he seems to be inheriting, is already familiar. As a baby he would crawl to his feet, stop at the sight of a pair of exceptionally large shoes, and let his gaze travel slowly upwards till recognition dawned.

Some of Diana's passion for children was obviously inherited from her father. He was deeply fond of his own brood, and he has already had the family camera snapping overtime on Prince William, as he once had on his mother. The Spencer grandchildren will learn Diana's family history from the treasures of Althorp, its ancestral portraits and its often told stories about children of the past, like naughty Sarah Spencer, who, in the last century, was punished by being locked up in the cupboard beneath the stairs. From that side of the family comes the Stuart blood. On the wrong side of the blanket they are descended from Charles II, the merry monarch whose legendary charm, love of finery, humour and ease of manner with his subjects seems to have been passed down to Diana. The history lessons for the royal children will be stuffed with the names of their relations, and with Charles around to explain it all to them (history was a particular favourite of his at school and he studied it at university) it should easily come alive.

But the Earl is determined that his grandchildren should have other centres to gather in than the grandeur of Althorp. With nostalgic memories of his own bucket-and-spade holidays, he has bought properties on a beach near Bognor in Sussex, so that they can holiday in two big adjacent houses, with the freedom of their own swimming pool and a beach within a pebble's throw. The informality of the seaside is something he thinks they ought to enjoy, though the houses have been carefully chosen so that they can be easily made secure and are not too vulnerable to cameras.

At first, to the Wales' children, the constant presence of cameras and of security men will be so familiar that it will be taken as a matter of course. It will be some while before the realisation dawns that other children are not followed by detectives with guns, or greeted by a sea of cameras at their front gate, and that not all babies are wheeled with walkie-talkies in their prams to summon help if it is needed. William had hardly begun to walk when he found an intriguing button in his nursery at Balmoral, and called out the local Scottish police hotfoot: never again, after the incident in 1982 in which Michael Fagan managed to reach The Queen's bedroom in Buckingham Palace, will an alarm summons be answered in a dilatory way. The police were not too distressed to discover the reason for their summons this time. 'Although it caused quite a panic, eventually everyone saw the funny side of it,' a detective was quoted as saying at the time. 'After all, the Prince is no different from any other child. Full of fun and curiosity.' Then William took it upon himself to test the reactions of the Metropolitan force by toddling through an infra-red beam in the walled garden at Kensington Palace. Another host of alarmed policemen suddenly appeared before his interested eyes. The significance of their presence will not dawn on these royal children for some time. But once it has, a degree of innocence and peace of mind must vanish.

For the childhood of these children will be more hedged about by security precautions and gadgetry than Charles' ever was. There were no armed marksmen disguised as outriders on The Queen's Coronation procession as there were on Charles' and Diana's wedding day. There was no precedent, before The Queen's visit to Jordan in 1984, of flying in an aircraft protected by anti-missile devices. Since the assassination of Charles' adopted grandfather, Earl Mountbatten, in 1979, no member of the Royal Family can have felt quite secure. This must have been Diana's worry when, weeping, she said goodbye to her husband on his way to the funeral of President Sadat of Egypt, assassinated so soon after their honeymoon meeting. And her children too must gradually learn to feel at the mercy of a sniper's bullet during every major royal event until the family are safely within doors again.

They will also learn that it is the unwritten rule in their family to act as if such fears do not exist. And they will learn that if 'incidents' do happen, as when their royal grandmother had a pistol waved at her while riding down the Mall in 1982, it is quite unthinkable to show any emotion in public. It will be explained to them that, while American presidents may surround themselves with guards, the British Royal Family have a rule that they do not allow fear for their security to prevent them being seen openly and easily.

Worries about personal safety and the irritating constraint of having detectives constantly at their sides, may not be as much of a handicap to the royal children as the attentions of the press. Prince Charles' adolescence was made agonizing at times by their persistence. When he was caught drinking cherry brandy under age, for example, he was branded a thoughtless and naive youngster in front of millions in early adolescence, just when it hurt most. Perhaps because of this early lack of consideration on the part of the press, Charles occasionally still loses his temper with journalists, even though he is one of the best of his family at handling them. He will sympathize with and understand his own

Below: For all the support and love around him, there will be times when Prince William must walk alone. This picture, taken at Kensington Palace, shows he is making a good start.

Above: The Picture Gallery at Althorp, seat of the Spencer family, where the Earl Spencer will no doubt delight in showing his grandchildren its treasures and telling them about their other family history.

Below: To help overcome his shyness, Prince William is shown how a camera works.

children's predicament, and give them an excellent example to follow, but he can do little to protect them from snooping cameras and upsetting stories. His wife is no less a victim. Even though early on she developed an almost jokey relationship with some of the most unscrupulous of royal journalists, she still finds the pressures almost impossible to bear at times. 'You- you- go away!' she shouted angrily at the posse of cameramen on her doorstep at Kensington Palace, in a moment of complete frustration and misery soon after William's birth.

She is aware that even her children's private moments of exhilaration may be exposed by long-distance lenses. It happened to her the day she danced outside her own front door with Prince Charles. She has discovered what it feels like to be proclaimed – without the right of reply – anorexic, childish, neurotic, on the verge of a nervous breakdown, spoilt, a girl who was making Charles' life a misery and, perhaps most hurtful of all, a girl who had, throughout her life, shown a pattern of just giving up when things got tough. The knowledge that she had done nothing to deserve the vitriol did not ease the hurt, especially as the slurs came at a time when she was finding the business of being a Royal difficult enough to cope with.

Despite the twin problems of publicity and security, the children of this generation of the Royal Family will never be shut away from the world as Charles and Anne and previous generations were. Peter Phillips, at a local day prep school near his parents' home in Gloucestershire is already enjoying a freedom only occasionally marred by the presence of cameras when he is with his grandmother The Queen at a horse show or a family outing. The Wales' children will spend less time in the privacy of their country home at Highgrove, because Charles' and Diana's work keeps them in London for most of the time, but both the

Prince and Princess are ingenious enough to devise ways of making their children familiar with the world outside the gates of Kensington Palace without attracting too much attention. Diana, despite her famous face, has not given up her trips round the shops, her calls into restaurants, her visits to her hairdresser's salon in public hours. Even The Queen sometimes manages to slip into Harrods through the back door and inspect the goods on display: a petite figure in a headscarf usually unrecognized by those who wait in the queues at the tills. Children change so quickly that it will be years before Diana's own can be easily recognized in public – particularly if the adult face beside them is unfamiliar. These children will not grow up unused to travelling by bus and tube and black cab like their father and grandmother. For Prince Charles and The Queen, these things were unimaginable treats. The existence of so many cousins and friends in their circle who do live very normal lives – Lady Sarah's daughter, for example – will help to prevent too much isolation, and too much protection from the reality of other people's lives. Prince Charles, who is especially interested in the problem areas of low employment and low income, is likely to make a special effort to introduce his children to a wider perspective than could be easily seen from within the Palace walls.

Even so, Charles' and Diana's children will find that they are in the uncomfortable position of being looked up to to set a good example. If they fail to consider the implications of any of their actions, they will be taken to task sharply. They will not be able to escape from the fact that the Royals set fashions, in behaviour as well as in clothes. With Prince William this happened from his very first appearance in public, when the fashion industry began to scrutinize his wardrobe. 'Prince William has changed babies' fashion overnight,' said the delighted managing director of a firm specializing in old-fashioned embroidered romper suits. William is also watched for the example he is setting in safety and health, in private as well as in public. Charles made this discovery when, on the private roads of a private estate in Balmoral he let his son sit on his lap and play with the steering wheel of his Range Rover, edging along at a mere 10 miles an hour. The news of the incident was leaked, and a shocked official from the Royal Society for the Prevention of Accidents denounced the practice as dangerous.

This family will have to live up to very high expectations, and it looks as though the Princess of Wales will do everything she can to help her children reach them. Already, through her charity work, and through consultations with medical practitioners and social service workers in the field, the Princess is beginning to develop her expertise on the subject of child care, health, safety, and the problems of rearing children in special circumstances. In the field of health Charles has demonstrated an interest in homeopathic and alternative medicine. Preventive medicine is another area in which the couple may play a special role. Already Diana is being praised as a mother who rarely drinks and never smokes, and it is known that she is very interested in healthy eating and exercise.

Charles and Diana will also be setting an example for others to follow in their choice of education for their children. Diana already has both practical and theoretical knowledge of play groups and nursery schools.

Above: The Queen, Prince Philip and Prince Charles will be on hand to guide the growing William when the time comes for him to take part in public duties. Nine days before the birth of her son, the Princess of Wales was with them on the balcony of Buckingham Palace to watch a flypast following the ceremony of Trooping the Colour.

The Young England nursery school follows the Montessori system, which was developed in Italy to encourage children to practise essential skills at their own pace. Diana's children are likely to benefit from this modern approach and enjoy opportunities denied to their father. Prince Charles has had a more thorough grounding for his job than any of his recent predecessors, but he knows that his parents and their advisors did make some mistakes. Charles was not happy at school and he is determined that his children should not suffer as he did. Royal children need more support from their home lives than most, and it is probable that the Wales' children will attend day schools for much longer than their father did.

To keep William near her as he grows, the Princess of Wales may argue in favour of the school her brother Charles attended, Eton, instead of remote Gordonstoun. Though it has the drawback of being within easy reach of Fleet Street, it has the immense advantage of being very close to Windsor and near enough to Central London for quick visits. Daughters of the couple are likely to be the first girls so close to the throne to be sent to mixed schools. They may, if they are academically minded, break another tradition and be the first royal girls to attend university. Both boys and girls are likely to spend part of their schooldays overseas, in Australia or Canada, or in Europe learning to ski and perfecting their French; knowledge of this language is essential for heirs to the throne. It is likely that Charles will ensure that there is some early coaching in Welsh in his children's education – Diana, who is learning the language, may sit in on the classes.

Outside the classroom, the children's own particular interests will doubtless be encouraged by a member of the Royal Family with specialist knowledge in the field. The list of royal skills is much longer than it has ever been. Nowadays young members of the Royal Family are not brought up exclusively to be soldiers, sailors or landowners. Lord Snowdon's career in photography has set an example for his son, who

Above left: Sometimes public duty can combine with personal delight. The Princess of Wales was thrilled to meet Rudolf Nureyev after a gala at the Royal Opera House, Covent Garden.
Above right: The Princess of Wales and Lady Sarah Armstrong-Jones relax together as spectators, while Prince Charles plays polo for England II against USA II in Windsor Great Park.

designs furniture. Lady Sarah Armstrong-Jones is interested in fine art. Princess Michael of Kent does interior decorating and writes books, so her children are likely to be encouraged to develop an artistic bent. Prince Richard, Duke of Gloucester, is a qualified architect. In the different houses of the Royal Family the Wales' children will find an exciting, varied, sometimes eccentric collection of people: sportsmen and racing drivers in Gatcombe Park; designers, opera singers and musicians at Princess Margaret's table; and, entertained in their own home, a wealth of guests: writers, such as William's own godfather, Sir Laurens van der Post; musicians and dancers – Diana is patron of the Welsh National Opera and is as besotted by ballet as Princess Margaret – academics, fashion designers, statesmen and sportsmen.

Despite the firm base of traditional values, and the traditional settings in which they will grow up, these children will also enjoy a wider freedom of choice and a more stimulating environment than the children of monarchs have for some centuries. Their home will be as secure and affectionate as their father and mother can make it – with the Prince and Princess of Wales there will be no danger of a loveless childhood, such as some of their ancestors were forced to suffer. And Diana will continue to provide the affectionate heart of that home life until the years, long distant, when the Children's Princess may at last accede to the title their great-grandmother has made so loved: Queen Mother.

She is one of the most famous women in the world. Yet the former Diana Spencer still feels most comfortable and natural in the company of children.

That's why, when she became the Princess of Wales, Diana began visiting schools, day care centers, and hospitals around the world. And, of course, she began her own wonderful family.

This delightful volume is filled with over 90 magnificent color photos of Princess Diana and adoring children from all over the world. Its text and pictures take you into the private family rooms of Kensington Palace and Highgrove House. Photos of Diana's maternity wardrobe, of the royal layette and much more provide a rare, intimate look at the close-knit family Princess Diana and Prince Charles have created.

A special section of this marvelous book features an endearing collection of children's drawings and comments – tributes to the Princess they adore.

The Horse Illustrated Guide to

Caring *for Your* Horse

BY LESLEY WARD